Engaging Pastors

Engaging Pastors
Papers and reflections from the Summative Conference
December 1–3, 2009

Jewel Gingerich Longenecker, editor

Church Leadership Center
Associated Mennonite Biblical Seminary

 *AMBS*

Institute of Mennonite Studies
Elkhart, Indiana

The Church Leadership Center at Associated Mennonite Biblical Seminary encompasses a variety of non-degree programs dedicated to the enrichment of current and future church leaders. By working together with AMBS faculty, Mennonite denominational leaders, district conference staff, and congregational leaders, the Church Leadership Center provides learning opportunities not available in the AMBS masters-level academic curriculum and offers ways for non-traditional students to benefit from AMBS's academic programs.

Published by Institute of Mennonite Studies
and the Church Leadership Center
of Associated Mennonite Biblical Seminary
Elkhart, Indiana 46517
© 2010 by Associated Mennonite Biblical Seminary

Second printing: December 2010
Printed in the United States of America by Evangel Press, Nappanee, Indiana

ISBN: 0-936273-45-3

Library of Congress Cataloging-in-Publication Data

Engaging Pastors Summative Conference (2009)
  Engaging Pastors papers and reflections from the Summative Conference
/ edited by Jewel Gingerich Longenecker ;Church Leadership Center,
Associated Mennonite Biblical Seminary.
      p. cm.
  "Published by Institute of Mennonite Studies and the Church Leadership
Center of Associated Mennonite Biblical Seminary"—T.p. verso.
  "December 1-3, 2009, Associated Mennonite Biblical Seminary hosted 103
church leaders for the Engaging Pastors Summative Conference"—Pref.
  ISBN 0-936273-45-3 (alk. paper)
  1. Clergy—Office—Congresses. 2. Mennonites—Clergy—Congresses. 3.
Pastoral theology—Mennonites—Congresses. 4. Christian
leadership—Mennonites—Congresses. I. Longenecker, Jewel Gingerich.
II. Associated Mennonite Biblical Seminary. Church Leadership Center.
III. Institute of Mennonite Studies (Elkhart, Ind.) IV. Title.
  BX8126.E54 2009
  262'.097--dc22
                          2010020767

15 14 13 12 11 10   10 9 8 7 6 5 4 3 2

Contents

  Both the practice and teaching of ministry are strengthened when pastors and professors regularly engage each other in ways that honor the knowledge and expertise of each.

Preface

On December 1–3, 2009, Associated Mennonite Biblical Seminary hosted 103 church leaders for the Engaging Pastors Summative Conference. The group consisted of denominational officials from Mennonite Church Canada and Mennonite Church USA, including executive leaders and conference ministers; educators and administrators from five of the six Mennonite institutions that offer pastoral education; and congregational pastors. All three sectors—denomination, educational institutions, and congregations—were nearly equally represented. All AMBS professors participated, along with several AMBS administrators. In addition, special guests Arthur Paul Boers, Steven Schweitzer, and David Wood attended, and AMBS professor emeritus Jacob Elias (now in a pastoral role) joined the group. The pages that follow include both the presentations from the Summative Conference and the fruits of our discussion.

To prepare for the conference, a small group of AMBS faculty read through the project reports gathered from Engaging Pastors projects over four and a half years, looking for recurring patterns and emerging themes. The following conclusions emerged, each representing an area of growth and learning for Mennonite seminaries and denominational leaders in the generation ahead:

1. Both the practice and teaching of ministry are strengthened when pastors and professors regularly engage each other in ways that honor the knowledge and expertise of each.

2. There is an urgent need and opportunity for pastoral, biblical, and teaching authority to be strengthened in the Mennonite church.

3. The church and the seminary need to equip pastors and professors to read and engage their missional contexts with joy.

The Summative Conference was planned as a working conference aimed at testing these conclusions. After an initial evening of orienting attendees to the project, sessions followed a pattern designed to maximize engagement. Each session began with the presentation of three brief reflection papers on a particular key learning. These were presented by representatives of each sector—a conference minister, a pastor, and a professor. Presenters responded to questions of whether and how this learning resonates in their settings, what we ought to pay attention to in it, and the implications of the learning for their work in the days ahead. Presenters were then invited to interact with one another around the content of their papers.

These presentations were followed by small group discussion. Prior to the conference participants were organized into working groups of five or six, with all three sectors—pastor, educator, and denomination—represented in each. Group members discussed questions regarding the session's key learning and provided written responses to a Listening Committee. The Listening Committee met between sessions to synthesize and analyze feedback. At the beginning of the next plenary session, the committee reported what they had heard from the working groups. This pattern continued throughout the event, covering all three key learnings.

Originally conference planners hoped to bring in a keynote speaker for opening night, in order to provide context for the Engaging Pastors project by hearing about other efforts aimed at deepening connections between seminaries and their sponsoring denominations and congregations. Claire Wolfteich of Boston University School of Theology agreed to provide the keynote speech. However, in early October Claire learned of a complication raised by her prior commitment to donate a kidney; she was now required to be present at a New York hospital for tests on the opening day of the conference. After a bit of scrambling on all sides, Claire agreed to join us instead by videoconference during the lunch hour the next day.

The conference culminated in a closing session designed to draw more intentionally on wisdom from the right side of the brain. After a thirty-minute period in which the Listening Committee summarized and commented on the issues raised by the Summative Conference, we asked participants to gather one more time in their working groups. Their final assignment was to distill their learnings from the week into some form of creative expression. While at first there were groans and misgivings, the session proved wonderfully joyful and fruitful. Attendees entered into the assignment through musical performances, drawings, poetry, drama, and more, offering several images for how the ecology of ministry in the Mennonite church might function differently and better in light of the learnings of the Engaging Pastors project.

Our initial sense is that the Summative Conference's impact on both the church and the seminary may be substantial. The event generated a great deal of energy and conversation among leaders. One long-time conference minister told us (with some dismay) that this was the first time in his memory that a group spanning these sectors—pastor, educator, and conference/denomination—had come together to discuss pastoral formation in the Mennonite church. He and many others called for structural changes to ensure that these kinds of conversations will become a regular part of our life together.

Jewel Gingerich Longenecker
Director, Engaging Pastors

Acknowledgments

Visionaries

Special thanks to J. Nelson Kraybill, Arthur Paul Boers, and Loren L. Johns for their roles in imagining and launching Engaging Pastors.

In mid-2004, then–AMBS President J. Nelson Kraybill found a Lilly Endowment Request for Proposals in his mailbox. The request called for the development of programs that would "help seminaries make connections that will strengthen the network of institutions essential for the calling, training, and sustaining of high-quality pastoral leadership." We thank Nelson for challenging AMBS to respond with interest to this request, for guiding the process of testing the project internally and externally, and for championing Engaging Pastors throughout the last five years of his presidency.

Arthur Paul Boers, then Associate Professor of Pastoral Theology at AMBS, led the process of developing and writing

11

the grant, working alongside a committee of faculty and administrators and guiding three summertime mini-colloquies that ultimately determined the shape of the Engaging Pastors project. He then went on to lead all four of the Engaging Pastors Pastor-Faculty Colloquies, co-led three Clarifying the Call events, met with several pastors on sabbatical, and participated in a day with conference ministers. He served on the oversight committee for four years. Arthur's involvement was vital to the success of Engaging Pastors and we are deeply grateful.

Loren Johns, AMBS Associate Professor of New Testament, played a pivotal role in the early stages of Engaging Pastors. As academic dean during the formation and launch of the grant, Loren was a key player in the planning and writing process. His enthusiasm and vision for the project laid an important foundation for Engaging Pastors' future. About midway through Engaging Pastors, Loren moved out of the dean's office into full-time teaching, but he continued to participate enthusiastically in Engaging Pastors activities.

Listening Committee

Thank you to the Listening Committee for its excellent work in hearing participants' thoughts, sifting through working group notes, and reporting thoughtfully and carefully in plenary sessions. Members were Megan Ramer, Pastor of Chicago Community Mennonite Church, Chicago, Illinois; Noel Santiago, Executive Minister for Franconia Mennonite Conference of Mennonite Church USA; Sara Wenger Shenk, Associate Dean and Associate Professor of Christian Practices at Eastern Mennonite Seminary, and President-Elect of AMBS; and Robert J. (Jack) Suderman, General Secretary of Mennonite Church Canada.

Summative Conference Planning Committee

We thank the following people for planning the Summative Conference: Lee Lever, Director, Denominational Ministry, Mennonite Church USA; Cyneatha Millsaps, Pastor, Community Mennonite Church, Markham, Illinois; Mary Schertz, AMBS Professor of New Testament; and Rebecca Slough, AMBS Academic Dean; as well as former members J. Nelson Kraybill and Arthur Paul Boers. Engaging Pastors staff serving on the planning committee included Jewel Gingerich Longenecker, Director; Nina Lanctot, Assistant Director; and Eric Saner, Administrative Assistant. The planning committee was a subset of the Engaging Pastors Oversight Committee, which also included George Brunk III, Interim President of AMBS; David Bergen, Executive Secretary, Christian Formation, Mennonite Church Canada; and Mary Lehman Yoder, Pastor, Assembly Mennonite Church, Goshen, Indiana.

Editorial staff

Thanks to Jen Stallings for compiling, copyediting, and formatting the Summative Conference papers, and to Barbara Nelson Gingerich, Managing Editor of Institute of Mennonite Studies, for expert editorial and publishing guidance.

Summative Conference participants

Finally, thanks to all who made the Summative Conference a rich experience through their participation: Darrell Baer, Rudy Baergen, Rafael Barahona, Lois Y. Barrett, Muriel Bechtel, David Bergen, Arthur Paul Boers, Wesley Bontreger, David W. Boshart, Richard Bowman, George R. Brunk III, Jeremiah Buhler, Owen E. Burkholder, J. Ron Byler, Iris de Leon–

Hartshorn, Timothy R. Detweiler, Irma Fast Dueck, Jacob W. Elias, Gilberto Flores, Dorothy J. Nickel Friesen, J. Stanley Friesen, David Gerber, Gerald Gerbrandt, Ronald D. Guengerich, Marco A. Guete, Matthew W. Hamsher, Tyler Hartford, Virginia Hooper, Garry W. Janzen, Loren L. Johns, Janeen Bertsche Johnson, Andrew S. Brubacher Kaethler, Edward J. Kauffman, Thomas E. Kauffman, Nancy L. Kauffmann, Douglas H. Kaufman, Lois Johns Kaufmann, Anita Yoder Kehr, Sharon D. Kennel, Linford D. King, Mary E. Klassen, Henry Kliewer, Noah S. Kolb, Gayle Gerber Koontz, Theodore J. Koontz, Karl Koop, Henry Krause, Marlene Y. Kropf, Timothy Kuepfer, Nina Bartelt Lanctot, Lawrence L. Lever, Jewel Gingerich Longenecker, Karen Martens Zimmerly, Donna Mast, Trakoon Y. Masyawong, Marianne M. Mellinger, Brenda Hostetler Meyer, Myrna M. Miller Dyck, Daniel Z. Miller, David B. Miller, Eugene N. Miller, Joel R. Miller, Cyneatha L. Millsaps, Charles T. Neufeld, Samuel A. Olarewaju, Ben C. Ollenburger, Ron Penner, Megan Ramer, Debra L. Ratzlaff, Clarence E. Rempel, John D. Rempel, Carlos Romero, Sebastiano Robert Rosa, Eileen K. Saner, Eric A. Saner, Noel Santiago, Walter W. Sawatsky, Mary H. Schertz, Daniel S. Schipani, Lynn M. Schlosser, Steven J. Schweitzer, James Shantz, Sara Wenger Shenk, Ryan L. Siemens, Heidi J. Siemens-Rhodes, Rebecca J. Slough, Arthur E. Smoker, Pauline F. Steinmann, J. Andrew Stoner, Ervin R. Stutzman, Robert J. Suderman, David L. Sutter, Janice Yordy Sutter, Warren L. Tyson, Isaac S. Villegas, Philip E. Waite, Herman Weaver, L. Keith Weaver, Claire Wolfteich (by video conference), David Wood, Jeff Wright, Don A. Yoder, Mary Lehman Yoder.

Opening address

Jewel Gingerich Longenecker

"Engaging Pastors will transform seminary-church connections through sustained interaction between professors and pastors. Our learnings will feed into our formation of pastors and serve as a primary vehicle for AMBS strategic planning even as we support the ecology of ministry." This bold claim serves as the mission statement for the Engaging Pastors project.

What exactly do we mean, you may wonder, by "ecology of ministry"? We've got a green library, a seminary garden, recycling, carbon offsets—and now an ecology of ministry? Is this some kind of faddish gobbledygook?

I admit that I thought so at first. And if you find this language confusing, please know that you are in good company.

Jewel Gingerich Longenecker is Associate Dean for Leadership Education at AMBS. In that role she directs the Church Leadership Center, including the Engaging Pastors project and other continuing education and non-degree programs.

At one point early in the grant period, the Engaging Pastors Oversight Committee—which is made up of such smart people as denominational leaders, professors, pastors, and the AMBS dean and president—was so confused by the phrase that they asked me to phone Lilly Endowment to find out exactly what it means. (You'll notice that none of them wanted to phone Lilly Endowment to ask this question—but of course, that is why we have staff!)

So I called. They told me something like this, which I found helpful:

> Lilly Endowment has several convictions about what is needed to support and sustain strong and vital congregations. The first is high-quality pastoral leadership. The second is theological education, which is absolutely pivotal. Third, there is a network of institutions that must work collaboratively in addressing challenges and in maintaining strong and vibrant religious communities.
>
> This network includes congregations, regional and national judicatories, colleges and universities, seminaries, independent agencies, retreat and conference centers, publishers, and other supporting organizations.

This network is the ecology of ministry.

Engaging Pastors was a concerted effort to create time and space for sustained conversations about ministry so that people from a range of points in the network—pastors, professors, and conference and denominational leaders—could learn from and benefit from these mutual exchanges and imagine new ways of working collaboratively. This week we gather to explore what these possibilities might be and their implications for our future together and in our various roles. Fundamentally, Engaging Pastors is concerned with helping these various parts of Mennonite Church USA and Mennonite Church Canada work better together to prepare and support pastors for the sake of sustaining strong and vital congregations. Needless to say, this is a good and important—even noble—goal.

Now for a confession: I have not always felt enthusiastic about the notion of this grant. In early 2004 when Nelson Kraybill, the AMBS president at the time, told me about a Request for Proposals he had received from Lilly Endowment, I groaned inwardly.

It's not that I didn't like Lilly or that I wasn't enthused about grants. To the contrary, I was feeling quite fond of Lilly at the time. Eighteen months earlier we had received a major grant to launch !Explore: A Theological Program for High School Youth. I was, quite frankly, exhausted. I had worked closely with the development of the !Explore grant, picking it up within a couple weeks of my arrival at AMBS, and I was relieved that finally after eighteen months, the director, Andy Brubacher Kaethler, had arrived on campus to launch the program. He was getting things off the ground well, and I figured that I could now turn my attention to the work I had really come here to do! I had a lot of plans, and none of them included writing one more report to Lilly Endowment.

It is a tribute to Lilly Endowment that I left Nelson's office half an hour later saying that I would keep an open mind. I read and re-read that Request for Proposals, looking for a fatal flaw. But it was hard to argue with the importance of this Making Connections Initiative, all summed up in the final sentence of the Request for Proposals: "This initiative seeks to help seminaries make connections that will strengthen the network of institutions essential for the calling, training, and sustaining of high-quality pastoral leadership."

It was even harder to argue with Nelson's main point to me—"Jewel, isn't this exactly what we said we wanted to do with a Church Leadership Center? Isn't this just providing funds for what we have wanted to make happen all along?"

In the end, Nelson and Lilly Endowment persuaded not just me but several of us on campus—and a number of people off campus—of the value of the Making Connections Initiative. Although we couldn't imagine doing one more thing, we saw how this grant could buy greater capacity for us to do the kind of connecting among pastors, denomination, and seminary that we sensed needed to happen but could not manage to do on limited budgets and with little discretionary time. And so a committee formed, a pilot project emerged, a proposal was written, and in December 2004 Lilly informed us that we would receive the $1.6 million we had requested.

What on earth can you do with that much money?

Well, you can do a lot. We decided that if we built in a lot of entry points, we would have a better chance of capturing the imagination of more people—of our own faculty and of pastors—and would increase the likelihood that people would want to be involved. Various people contributed their ideas for how professors might engage pastors, and in the end we had ten separate programs within the larger Engaging Pastors grant. Administratively ten is plenty, but in terms of generating interest, I think ten has been just about right. Each program has had its own unique benefits and its own champions among faculty. On the other hand, as time went on, several of the programs began to learn from each other, and soon some of them started to look very much alike and even become almost indistinguishable. We sometimes scratch our heads and say, "Now is that a study group or a colloquy? Or is that a course revision?" It's not all-important for you to keep the distinctions between these programs clearly in mind, but I would like to share photos that show a bit about what each one has aimed to accomplish:

1. **Clarifying the Call:** Sharing the joys and challenges of beginning pastoral ministry. Pastors in their first assignments came together with faculty and denominational ministers for support and learning.

2. **Pastor-Faculty Colloquy:** Discussing issues of leadership in the Mennonite church. Pastors and professors met to reflect on and study issues of ministry. Each year, the colloquy group met three times for extended conversations.

3. **Pastor Sabbatical:** Taking time for reflection, study, and rejuvenation. Church leaders spent time at AMBS for reflection and study. Research projects from these sabbaticals are available to professors and students.

4. **Pastor-Faculty Study Groups:** Studying together and refreshing spirits. Pastors and professors met together multiple times over several months to study the Bible or other issues of ministry.

5. **Seminary Course Revision:** Bringing pastoral experience into the seminary classroom. Pastors and professors collaborated to revise courses and sometimes to co-teach courses.

6. **Listening Project:** Visiting new pastors in their congregations to listen and learn. Professors learned from the congregation in its context and from the pastor, helping to understand how to better prepare pastors.

7. **Pastoral Habits Research Project:** Reflecting on what creates excellence in church leadership. Researchers interviewed exemplary pastors to learn characteristics of effective leaders.

8. **Connections with Conference, Area Church, and Denominational Ministers:** Collaborating to prepare and support pastors. Conference ministers, area church ministers, and denominational ministers participated in a variety of the Engaging Pastors programs.

9. **Seminario Bíblico Anabautista:** Helping the church broaden pastoral education and resources. Professors traveled to Dallas to participate in Spanish seminary classes, and seminario students visited AMBS in November 2009.

10. **Summative Conference:** Sharing findings and continuing the conversation. Denominational and conference leaders, educators, and pastors gather to test learnings from the Engaging Pastors project and to determine what structural changes can help us better prepare, support, and nurture pastors.

These were the programs of Engaging Pastors. After each engagement, we received reports from participating faculty, and in some cases, from pastors as well. As someone who is charged with reading all of these reports, please let me assure you that it is almost mind-boggling how many of these pastor-professor conversations have occurred over five years, and I can certainly attest to the transformative power of these conversations for both professors and pastors.

At the end of the fourth year, several other people read the reports, looking for recurring themes and repeated questions and issues. The three themes we've identified for this event grew out of this sifting process. While the themes certainly are not the only things we could discuss, it was our sense that these three themes were among the most commonly stated and among the most urgent.

We called this gathering because we want to test these themes with you. Do they resonate in your experience? If so, how? We have planned this event to give maximum time for you to speak back to us about your experiences in relation to these themes, and we are extremely eager to hear what you have to say.

Before I wrap this up, I want to bring you up to date on one more thing. While Engaging Pastors and !Explore are technically unrelated, I can't help but see a lot of ways they have reinforced each other and have together energized AMBS in recent years. For that reason, I want to share with you tonight that there are important changes happening with !Explore.

Recently we began to reconsider how !Explore is positioned within AMBS's life and structure. While up to now !Explore has been an important non-degree program, it has had minimal impact on seminary students. This is unfortunate, because in listening to what is happening in the lives of pastors and congregational members, we at AMBS have become increasingly attuned to the need for greater attention to matters of faith formation and culture, matters near and dear to the !Explore program. While in some important informal ways, learning from !Explore has seeped back into the classroom, no formal avenue has existed to harness that learning for the sake of students preparing for ministry.

So, this fall we decided to launch an effort to integrate learnings from !Explore into the life and experience of seminary students through the formation of a Center for Faith Formation and Culture, of which !Explore will be one part. A Center for Faith Formation and Culture will endow a teaching faculty position for someone who will champion these concerns, and it will formally make a place for the concerns of faith formation and culture in our curriculum. Over the next eighteen months we will be fundraising toward a $2.5 million endowment to support this Center for Faith Formation and Culture.

I am happy to report tonight that Lilly Endowment recently awarded us a new grant to be used toward this endowment. Because we requested the maximum of $500,000 for this purpose, we were surprised and thrilled to receive not $500,000, but $600,000 from Lilly Endowment toward our goal.

This move toward a Center for Faith Formation and Culture is one step in a major curricular review process now underway at AMBS. We expect other new directions and initiatives to grow out of this curricular review and are looking to this event—the Engaging Pastors Summative Conference—to feed that process in a substantial way.

Thank you very much for joining us for this event. I look forward to our interactions these next two days.

EP photo captions

Clarifying the Call
Arthur Paul Boers (center), AMBS associate professor of pastoral theology, leads a discussion with pastors at Clarifying the Call in 2009. Participants included Steven Cox, Niagara United Mennonite Church, Niagara on the Lake, ON; Craig Oury, Mount Zion Mennonite Church, Boonsboro, MD; Jeff Linthicum, Pine Creek Chapel, Arcadia, FL. (Photo by Mary E. Klassen)

Yoel Masyawong, pastor of Grace Lao Mennonite Church, Kitchener, ON, receives a blessing from his congregation, shared by Rebecca Slough, AMBS academic dean, at Clarifying the Call, March 2009. (Photo by Mary E. Klassen)

Pastor-Faculty Colloquy
Participating in the first Pastor-Faculty Colloquy in 2005–2006 were (beginning from center front) Carolyn Collins and Keith Collins, Church of the Overcomer, Trainer, PA; Rebecca Slough, AMBS professor of worship and the arts; Samuel Lopez, administrator of the Spanish Mennonite Council of Churches and bishop of Lancaster Mennonite Conference; Mag Richer Smith and Bob Smith, First Mennonite Church, Iowa City, IA; Jacob Elias, AMBS professor of New Testament; Doug Luginbill, Hope Mennonite Church, Wichita, KS. Additional participants not included in the photo were Gayle Gerber Koontz, AMBS professor of theology and ethics; Arthur Paul Boers, AMBS associate professor of pastoral theology; Craig Maven, then pastor at First Mennonite Church, Berne, IN; and David Wood, facilitator. (Photo by Mark Shephard)

The 2006–2007 Colloquy focused on teaching the Bible in the congregation and one session was held at a retreat center in Idaho where Eugene Peterson, author and creator of "The Message" version of The Bible, participated in discussions. Arthur

Paul Boers, to Peterson's left, was a facilitator of all the Colloquy sessions. (Photo by Mary E. Klassen)

Pastor Sabbatical

Pastors on sabbatical at AMBS in April 2009 joined with several local pastors and members of the AMBS community to discuss ministry in diverse settings. Discussion and prayer included in one cluster Samuel Olarewaju from Berean Fellowship, Youngstown, OH; Rob Burdette, then transitional pastor at Hively Avenue Mennonite Church, Elkhart; and Loren Johns, AMBS professor of New Testament; and in another cluster Nina Lanctot, AMBS assistant director of Engaging Pastors; Angela Nze from Christ Life Chapel, Avondale, AZ; and Seferina deLeon from Iglesia Menonita del Buen Pastor, Goshen. (Photo by J. Tyler Klassen)

Sheldon Burkhalter, conference minister for Pacific Northwest Conference, spent six weeks of his sabbatical at AMBS, working on a project, "Old and New Mennonites Together for a Revitalized Church," examining how people new to the Mennonite church and those from traditional Mennonite congregations might strengthen each other. During his time at AMBS, Burkhalter was able to participate in a prayer walk that also included Richard Rohr (holding cross), founding director of Center for Action and Contemplation, Albuquerque, NM. (Photo by Mary E. Klassen)

Study group

Mary Schertz (near the fireplace at the back), professor of New Testament, led several Pastor-Faculty Study Groups, including one on the release texts in Luke. Each session involved reading the text confessionally, time for creating an artful response, and worship. (Photo by Mary E. Klassen)

The 2005–2006 Pastor-Faculty Study Group involved women pastors, including three from Goshen: Klaudia Smucker, then at College Mennonite Church; Lois Johns Kaufmann at Assembly Mennonite Church, Goshen; and Loanne Harms on the pastoral team at Waterford Mennonite Church. (Photo by Mary E. Klassen)

Seminary course revision

David Hendricks (left), pastor of Prince of Peace Church of the Brethren in South Bend, IN, was invited by Steve Schweitzer, assistant professor of Old Testament, to collaborate in teaching the course, "From Daniel to Jesus: Early Judaism in the Second Temple Period." Members of the class included Ron Kennel, Christina Litwiller, Janet Rasmussen, and Ruth Harder. (Photo by Mary E. Klassen)

Listening Project

Lois Siemens and Superb Mennonite Church, Kerrobert, SK, hosted Mary Schertz, professor of New Testament, for a Listening Project visit in April 2009.

Gayle Gerber Koontz, AMBS professor of theology and ethics, spent a weekend with Cincinnati (OH) Mennonite Church and pastor Joel Miller, learning more about the congregation, its ministries in the city, and how AMBS can better prepare pastors for the early years of ministry.

Conference ministers
Conference Ministers and Area Church Ministers extended their annual meetings in December 2006 to discuss issues of how seminaries can better train pastors and how the church can better sustain pastors in congregational ministry. Diane Zaerr Brenneman, then on the ministerial staff of Mennonite Church USA; Jim Pankratz, Conrad Grebel University College; and Loren Johns, AMBS professor of New Testament, confer at a break in these discussions. (Photo by Eric Saner)

Seminario
Seminario Bíblico Anabautista students were hosted at AMBS in fall 2009 as a way to build connections between the two groups of graduate-level students and faculty. After a chapel service in which the Spanish-speaking pastors described their congregations and AMBS students and faculty described seminary worship experiences, the Seminario group posed for a photo with their instructors. In the front row are Blanca Vargas, Alberto Parchmont, Aurora Parchmont, Juan Limones, Oneida Dueñas, and Samuel Moran. Behind them are Nina Bartelt Lanctot, assistant director of Engaging Pastors; Daniel Schipani, AMBS professor of pastoral care and counseling; Lois Barrett; director of AMBS–Great Plains; and José Ortiz, instructor of the course in Christian worship. (Photo by Mary E. Klassen)

In a class taught by José Ortiz at AMBS, Oneida Dueñas of Ferris, TX, talks about issues of worship in her congregation. Aurora Parchmont, Juan Limones, and Samuel Moran also participated, along with several AMBS faculty and administrators who sat in to learn from the students. (Photo by Mary E. Klassen)

Keynote speech

Claire Wolfteich

I am glad to be here to address you today and to have the opportunity for conversation. The Engaging Pastors initiative of Associated Mennonite Biblical Seminary has done tremendous work in fostering serious and sustained dialogue and collaboration among seminary professors, students, pastors, and denominational leaders. I found it inspiring to read about the work you all have done together. At Boston University, we have engaged in some quite similar endeavors: colloquies among faculty and pastors, curricular revision, field visits, reflections on excellence in ministry—though these all take on different contours in our different

Claire Wolfteich is Associate Professor of Practical Theology and Spiritual Formation at Boston University School of Theology, where she also co-directs the Center for Practical Theology. She has served as President of the Association of Practical Theology and Vice President of the International Academy of Practical Theology. She is the author of several books, including Sabbath in the City: Sustaining Urban Pastoral Excellence, which she co-authored with Bryan Stone.

contexts. As there are important intersections with our own work at Boston University, and as we each also make some distinctive contributions, I find it hopeful and generative to explore what we each have learned. Today I want to share with you some of the key findings of our work at Boston University, focusing particularly on points that resonate and confirm the key learnings of Engaging Pastors as well as several points of difference in our approaches, contexts, and learning. Through this conversation, I hope that we each will move to clearer and more creative visions for the next steps of our work.

The three key learnings of the Engaging Pastors program bear repeating:

1. Both the practice and teaching of ministry are strengthened when pastors and professors regularly engage each other in ways that honor the knowledge and expertise of each.

2. There is an urgent need and opportunity for pastoral, biblical, and teaching authority to be strengthened in the Mennonite church.

3. The church and the seminary need to equip pastors and professors to read and engage their missional contexts with joy. "How can Mennonite pastors become effective analysts of their contexts and joyful evangelists of the gospel?"

I will explore these as I tell some of the story of our work in Boston. Let me begin with our strong confirmation of your first learning. At Boston University, we have learned so much through our work with pastors and other religious leaders.

In several Lilly Endowment grant projects over the past ten years, we have partnered with pastors, congregations, and denominational leaders to think about how we do spiritual and pastoral formation, to design innovative new courses, to teach together, to jointly do research, and to sustain excellence in urban ministry. In 2005, this work led to the establishment of the Center for Practical Theology at Boston University, funded with generous support from Lilly Endowment. My colleague Bryan Stone and I co-direct the center. The Center for Practical Theology seeks to provide a bridge between the scholarly resources, questions, and insights of a university-based theological seminary and the wisdom, questions, and traditions of communities of faith. In doing so, the center provides an infrastructure for sustaining, deepening, and expanding important relationships and connections between Boston University School of Theology and local congregations, denominational offices, and religious centers so that they may be more integrally incorporated into student learning and faculty teaching and research. Like you, we have learned that such partnerships are mutually beneficial.

Reading contexts of ministry:
Pastors and seminary faculty working together

Let me give a few examples to put flesh on these abstract bones. For the past five years, Bryan Stone and I co-directed a project called Sustaining Urban Pastoral Excellence (SUPE). In a sense, our project represented our own reading of our missional context. As Bryan wrote in the book we co-authored, *Sabbath in the City: Sustaining Urban Pastoral Excellence*:

The Boston University campus snakes its way through the city of Boston, with the Charles River at our backs and the hustle and bustle of Commonwealth Avenue and a busy trolley line right outside our front doors. We wanted to be more intentional as a school about how we respond to the urban environment in the ways we teach, learn, and conduct research. For despite the fact that the vast majority of pastors minister in urban contexts today, ministerial education still operates as if the city has very little impact on the way ministry is carried out or on the way pastors are prepared for ministry. . . . The urban context *should* affect what seminaries teach and how they teach.[1]

The project on Sustaining Urban Pastoral Excellence was an attempt to analyze the urban context and to explore how pastors can live out their callings in the city. It was designed both as a program of support to urban pastors and as a research project, which sought answers to two primary questions: (1) what *constitutes* pastoral excellence in the urban context, and (2) what *sustains* it? The project focused on four key areas that we originally hypothesized as contributing to healthy and vibrant ministry in the city: partnership, spiritual renewal, sabbath, and study.

1. **Partnership.** Pastors frequently say they experience isolation. At the heart of the program, therefore, were four-member partnerships consisting of pastoral leaders from

---

1. Bryan P. Stone and Claire E. Wolfteich, *Sabbath and the City: Sustaining Urban Pastoral Excellence* (Louisville, KY: Westminster John Knox Press, 2008), xi. (Portions of this address were previously published in *Sabbath and the City* and have been reprinted here by permission of the publisher.)

the same city, who applied to the program together. During the six-month cycle in which they participated, the pastors met biweekly for fellowship, support, accountability, study, renewal, and sharing. These partnerships—which we came to frame as holy friendships—provided much-needed safe space for the expression of vulnerabilities and for spiritual companioning, outside the sometimes competitive denominational group gatherings. Here our work very much corroborated your own. As Arthur Paul Boers, one of your colloquy facilitators, wrote: "I am impressed by how lonely pastoring can be. . . . This reinforced the priority of emphasizing collegiality in pastoring."

2. **Spiritual renewal.** Each of the partnerships developed plans for their own spiritual renewal during the six-month cycle, including individual and group practices integrated with their biweekly meetings and sabbatical leave time. We invited pastors to envision what spiritual renewal would mean, and we offered theological and biblical frameworks for thinking about spiritual renewal.

3. **Sabbath.** Urban pastors easily experience burnout and exhaustion in the absence of healthy, biblical rhythms of work, play, rest, and renewal. The project funded sabbatical leave time for each pastor and was instrumental in helping them focus on flexible, creative, and sustainable sabbath practices such as art, recreation, journaling, prayer, travel, reading, and fellowship that help bring balance and wholeness to life and ministry. I will say

more about sabbath later in my address, for this became a critical part of our learning.

4. **Study.** Each partnership identified one key question to pursue in depth during their cycle of participation—a question of interest to the entire group and representative of the issues or questions that each pastor faces in his or her own unique urban environment. Some of the study questions focused on immigration, violence and peacemaking, multicultural ministry, clergy and church "divides," congregational growth and decline in the urban context, race and reconciliation, art as means of healing clergy divisions, spiritual growth in the desert, and urban networking. Here I was interested in a difference in our approaches. At AMBS, your joint Pastor-Faculty Study Groups seemed to involve substantial faculty commitment and the study topics seemed directed by the faculty research area. Pastors appeared to participate energetically. At Boston University, the pastoral partnerships identified their own study question arising from their own particular contexts of ministry. While we helped to refine the question, develop an approach, and identify resources, the pastors met biweekly on their own to study together. We gained quite a bit in learning what questions the pastors identified as needing study. Too often, academics determine the direction of research and study in a vacuum. So, for us, this was a refreshing and empowering change. On the other hand, we found that we had overestimated pastors' time and interest in study or research. While many pastors craved more time for reading, the charge of biweekly study sometimes seemed like

a burden and even at odds with our simultaneous call for spiritual renewal and sabbath. I think this reflected pastors' work overload. It also reflected the clash that may occur when the academic mindset imposes itself on the realities of pastoral life (for example, we began thinking that pastors would conduct "research," then changed to "study," and for most the reality was "reading.") More troubling, though, is the possibility that we have lost an ability to portray study as a spiritual practice and one essential to sustaining excellence in ministry. Our work on this project leads us now to emphasize the connections between spirituality and study in our initiatives around curricular revision and spiritual formation at the School of Theology.

One of the most basic things we learned through our project was that excellent pastors love the communities they serve. Here our findings resonate strongly with yours. Ted Koontz, a participant in your 2008–2009 colloquy, expressed this idea beautifully: "I am struck by the necessity of a pastor or a prophet to love the people to whom he or she speaks. . . . I'm convinced that the ability to love the sometimes unlovable must be rooted in knowing ourselves as the beloved. Pastoral excellence depends upon renewing that knowledge."

In our project, this meant loving not only the people in one's congregation but also loving their context—loving the city, with all its lovable and unlovable parts. Pastors certainly need skills and knowledge to interpret their changing contexts. I would venture to say that they also need to love a context to read it well and generously. Part of our work in formation, then, involves not just teaching social-scientific skills and giving theological frameworks for reading a context, but also cultivating the capacity to love. I concur with Koontz that love of others depends on true self-knowledge—knowledge of oneself as a beloved creation of God. For me, this means that reading a context must include reading the self, and that spiritual formation goes hand in hand with knowing communities and developing interpretive skill.

Over five years, we worked with ninety-six urban pastors. Our partnerships represented an amazing cross-section of the United States: Aurora, Illinois; Baltimore, Maryland; Bangor, Maine; Birmingham, Alabama; Boston, Massachusetts; Bridgeport, Connecticut; Chattanooga, Tennessee; Chicago, Illinois; El Paso, Texas; Hampton Roads, Virginia; Hartford, Connecticut; Los Angeles, California; New York, New York; Portland, Oregon; Salt Lake City, Utah; San Diego, California; Savannah, Georgia; Seattle, Washington; Springfield, Connecticut; and Syracuse, New York. We visited every site, sharing in their worship services, exploring the local communities, listening to the pastors and their congregations. We were able to offer scholarly resources and knowledge (both theological and social-scientific) to aid the pastors in interpreting their contexts, identifying the most pressing questions, and developing a manageable approach to learning what they needed to learn. At the same time, we learned so much from seeing the contexts with the pastors. Here there is great resonance with the Listening Project of the Engaging Pastors grant. Indeed, I am fascinated by the possibilities of continuing such field visits with recent alumni, and expanding the participants to include a broader section of the faculty.

I also am intrigued by the possibilities that emerge when we involve pastoral leaders more directly in the envisioning, revisioning, design, and teaching of courses. This is something we share: both our work in Boston and your work here at AMBS found that pastors bring important insights to what, and more importantly, *how* we teach.

I read with interest about your experiences here at AMBS in jointly working on courses across a range of theological disciplines: From Daniel to Jesus, and Teaching the Bible in the Congregation, to Human Sexuality and Christian Ethics, and Foundations of Worship and Preaching. For the past five years, the Center for Practical Theology has facilitated a Curricular Innovation and Redesign process. This has been an exciting way to connect faculty with pastoral leaders in order to take a fresh look at our teaching. The process pairs faculty with pastoral leaders for a semester of small group and large group meetings around rethinking pedagogy, selection of texts, course aims, and how we contextualize our courses in light of students' vocational directions and the realities of faith communities.

Here is a sampling of the many courses we redesigned: John Hart, Professor of Christian Ethics, teamed up with two local pastors to redesign his course Christianity and Ecology in Community Context. Carole Bohn and James Burns, both of whom teach in the area of religion and psychology, worked as a faculty team together with Rev. LaTrelle Easterling, an African American female pastor, and Rev. Hyuk Seonwoo, a Korean American male pastor, to revamp the course Social Identity and Oppression. James Walters, New Testament professor, worked with pastoral partners to redesign the Introduction to New Testament course so that it could attend more intentionally to the disparate vocational needs of MDiv students preparing for ministry, on the one hand, and MTS students building an academic foundation for future doctoral studies, on the other hand. We also expanded our circle of partners to include a local imam and rabbi, who collaborated with Andrew Shenton, Assistant Professor of Sacred Music, on a new course entitled Music in World Religions.

The dynamic of the discussions brought us to important and honest conversation about the distinctive role of the academy in forming religious leaders, the limitations of the academy in forming religious leaders, and the ways in which congregations and universities can gain from one another wisdom about teaching. We also were drawn to discussions about spiritual practice and community in the context of classroom and congregation. What sorts of practices are necessary to knowing the subject matter? How are practices introduced authentically in a pluralistic, academic classroom setting? It is critical to sustain such collaborative curricular work—respecting the distinctive gifts of professors and pastors as well as the particularity of our respective contexts.

We also learned that pastors serve as important partners in the classroom. Our pastor-teacher program works with selected pastors in designing their own courses and teaching them. Here pastors bring immediate contact with congregational contexts and experience in ministry directly to the classroom. Pastors have taught courses such as Jazz of Preaching, Spirituality and Multi-Cultural Ministry, Spiritual Resources and Disciplines, and Enjoying the Pastoral Life. The Center for Practical Theology also has supported a pastor-scholar program, which invites pastors to take regular School of Theology courses for a nominal fee. Faculty across the disciplines have found it stimulating to have pastors in our courses alongside ministry students, bringing their experiences and congregational contexts to the subject matter, keeping alive questions of vocation and ministry at every turn.

One further way we sought to integrate pastoral wisdom and imagination into the regular work of faculty is through our faculty research grants in practical theology. In awarding the funding, we give priority to projects that display a practical, multidisciplinary, theological approach; that bring faculty and pastoral leaders into dialogue; and that attend to congregational contexts. Some of the research projects we supported included:

- Theologizing in the Aftermath: Resources for Religious Leaders Responding to Trauma—Dr. Shelly Rambo (Theology).

- The Development of an Integrated Field Education Program in the Korean Context—Dr. Hee An Choi (Director, Anna Howard Shaw Center) and Rev. Samuel M. Johnson (Director, Office of Professional Education)

- Clergy and Clinicians Interface Project—Dr. James Burns (Religion and Psychology)

- Moderate Christians with Liberal and Evangelical Instincts: Using a Web-Based Resource to Understand the Interests and Needs of an Under-Served Community, in order to Support their Faith and Learning—Dr. Wesley J.

Wildman (Theology) and Rev. Dr. S. Chapin Garner (Senior Pastor, Norwell United Church of Christ)

• Feminist and Womanist Practical Theology—Dr. Mary Elizabeth Moore (Dean of the School of Theology) and Dr. Shelly Rambo (Theology)

Pastoral excellence

Reflection on the second learning of the Engaging Pastors project highlights the importance of context in theological education. As a denominational seminary, AMBS can speak specifically to the needs of your faith community: "There is an urgent need and opportunity for pastoral, biblical, and teaching authority to be strengthened in the Mennonite church." At Boston University School of Theology, we have a strong identity as a United Methodist seminary and yet also operate within a pluralistic university context, with much denominational and interfaith diversity within the School of Theology. Thus, the questions of how to define the pastoral role are complex indeed, as we are preparing students for leadership in any number of denominations. And yet, in our work with pastors my colleague Bryan Stone and I came to embrace the term *excellence*, when understood as virtue (stemming from the Greek *arête*). When considered in this light, we might ask: What are the virtues intrinsic to the vocation to ministry? Where do we learn of these virtues in the scriptures and in our traditions? What sort of authority do these virtues carry, or rather, how is the authority of the pastor grounded in these virtues? I would assert that the strengthening of pastoral authority may rest in this sort of countercultural embrace of excellence understood as virtue. Our task, then, is to identify and cultivate the habits and practices that form excellent pastors, embodying the virtues of ministry in God's service.

The gift of the sabbath: Joy and excellence in ministry

One practice we found intrinsic to urban pastoral excellence is the practice of sabbath keeping. While this practice takes on particular importance in urban contexts, it is also critical to ministry in suburban and rural contexts. I will take some time here to unfold what we learned about sabbath, for this has been enormously important to our work. When we began the project, we offered pastors what we called an enrichment leave. Quickly we saw that this term did not capture the deeper spiritual sense that we sought to convey. We renamed the leave a sabbatical, and then came to frame sabbatical more and more explicitly in theological terms as sabbath—a time of spiritual rest, renewal, and re-creation.

In biblical texts about sabbath, two themes emerge as central motifs: creation and liberation. The first emphasizes sabbath as a time of awed respect for God as Creator and for the wonder of the created world, an imitation of the divine rhythm of creation and rest, work and sabbath. Biblical texts clearly link sabbath to the creation story: "So God blessed the seventh day and hallowed it, because on it God rested from all the work that he had done in creation" (Gen. 2:3; NRSV). At the same time, sabbath observance recalls Yahweh's liberation of the Jewish people from slavery: "Observe the sabbath day and keep it holy, as the LORD your God commanded you. . . . Remember that you were a slave in the land of Egypt, and the LORD your God brought you out from there with a mighty hand and an outstretched arm; therefore the LORD your God commanded you to keep the sabbath day" (Deut. 5:12, 15; NRSV).

Exodus 20:10 extends the sabbath command to the entire household, including slaves and animals, as well as resident aliens of the town. Sabbath represents freedom and justice for all creation, recognition of the dignity of all created beings. Jewish theologian Abraham Joshua Heschel writes, "The seventh day is the exodus from tension, the liberation of man from his own muddiness, the installation of man as a sovereign in the world of time."[2] The treatment of sabbath in the Gospels of Matthew and Mark reinforces a liberating understanding of sabbath and portrays Jesus as a fairly liberal interpreter of the sabbath command.

We found that this time of sabbath was incredibly important, sometimes life-changing, for the pastors. Often those themes of creation, re-creation, and freedom surfaced in the pastors' reflections. Connie Wells, a United Church of Christ pastor in a gritty section of Bangor, Maine, spent part of her sabbatical out in the southwest part of the United States. When she saw the wide open spaces of the Arizona desert, she realized how tired she was. She described the experience:

> Being touched by the timeless winds of Arizona was like living in the presence of the deep, wide, constant, and embracing Holy Spirit. The space of it gave me appreciation for God's creating, loving presence in all creation. . . . The most amazing part for me was dar-

---

2. Abraham Joshua Heschel, *The Sabbath* (New York: Farrar, Strauss, and Giroux, 1951), 29.

ing, trusting once again, to open myself to that God's presence. I realized how wary, weary, and shut down one can become in urban pastoral ministry.

For some, sabbatical was an invitation to creativity, an opportunity to reclaim oneself, and to remember one's vocation. Cliff Warner, an Episcopal priest in El Paso, spoke about sabbatical as providing space to remember who one is as an individual: "[It helped in] reconnecting with who I am as an individual—apart from the congregational pressures on identity formation/perception. . . . There are aspects of who I am that are not supported by the congregation (nor are they opposed, by the way). That part of me tends to fade away unless I have space to remember."

The process of developing sabbath practices, however, was also quite challenging for some urban pastors, and those more difficult experiences also shed light on urban ministry and spirituality in contemporary culture. Some found sabbatical to be too abrupt a shift from their usual habits of work (in their words, workaholism). Some felt adrift without their identity as pastor. Others struggled to negotiate boundaries with congregations. And while pastors' sabbaticals often yielded newly empowered lay leadership within the congregation, pastors did not always find it a smooth transition back to the pulpit. Grace Bartlett of Bangor wrote: "I have come to realize that the congregation for the most part does not recognize how demanding and stressful urban ministry can be. In fact it seems that the world at large and the congregational demands work at cross purposes to such renewal. It is countercultural to take sabbath/sabbatical breaks in a world that values and rewards the Protestant work ethic."

And yet, the liberation of the sabbath, its release from the exhaustion and productivity treadmill, enabled pastors to do ministry with excellence and joy. Claudia Rowe, a pastor in Portland, Oregon, related how her sabbatical affected her ministry. She traveled to Alaska and described a resonance between the expanse of the natural landscape and God's expansive generosity. Echoing Connie Wells's reflections in Arizona, she said that her sabbatical "was an experience of bathing in the generosity of God and God's love. . . . The transformative power of the experience of this goodness of God, in which I have believed, will be ongoing. I long to respond to people out of that endless generosity, rather than out of the sense of straightened resources that stress often produces in my psyche."

Again, the pastors' insights and experiences moved and shaped faculty learning as much as the faculty shaped the pastors' learning. This project deepened my own interest in the theology and practice of sabbath—a topic I had approached earlier through my writing in the area of work and faith. But the pastors brought the practice alive in my own life. To see these hard-working, dedicated pastors reach a point of pause—a pause that grew into life-sustaining, life-animating space and led one pastor to reflect on his busyness in ministry and name it idolatry—it stopped me in my tracks. How will I be sustained? Whose work am I doing? How do I practice sabbath as a university professor—and as a mother of three young children, whose needs do not stop so I can take a day apart?

My own experiences intersected with reflection on our students. How are they being formed for ministry? Where do they learn a healthy rhythm of work and rest? Where will they find joy in their ministry—a sense of creative grace sustaining them amid the endless urgent needs of others, meetings, funerals, sermon writing, family needs, shifting community contexts, and their own ebbs and flows of energy? We sense through our work that sabbath is a key to joy in ministry. We know that practices of sabbath keeping are constitutive of excellence in ministry.

So, this learning, gained with and for the church, flows back into our work as a faculty in the School of Theology. Our current grant project focuses on bringing the lessons from the work with urban pastors to inform the formation, mentorship, and teaching of ministry students. This entails curricular and co-curricular initiatives, including: (a) the development of partnerships with field education congregations specifically committed to the nurture of sabbath practices in student-pastors; (b) plenary sessions involving faculty, pastors, and students as part of the pastoral and spiritual formation program; (c) a conference about sabbath, co-sponsored with the Lord's Day Alliance; (d) spiritual renewal opportunities for students, including Reading Retreats and a weekly Sabbath Space that offers students a space and regular time for rest, fellowship, and creative activities in the middle of the busiest day on campus (these initiatives designed by doctoral student Susan Forshey); and (e) a new course entitled Sabbath: Theology and Practice, which I team taught with a Jewish rabbi.

Conclusion: Insights, challenges, visions, proposals

Some of the practices that we have learned are essential to pastoral excellence include, then, sabbath keeping, friendship, study, and regular habits of spiritual renewal. We have learned that pastors need early on as ministerial students to develop these habits, practices, rhythms, and relationships, or they may never develop them at all. Too often the seminary experience fails to model and reinforce them, and in fact models a way of life that is likely to lead to burnout, dysfunction, and a diminished sense of joy and vocation in pastoral ministry.

Thus, we are focusing attention on developing these practices in sustainable ways, early on in ministry formation and continuing with strong support particularly in the first five years of ministry. If the church is to take the city seriously as sacred space, it must have leaders who not only love the city and its people but also have acquired the knowledge, skills, and virtues necessary for urban ministry. They have to know how to read and interpret contexts as well as texts, for both may be revelatory of God. They need to know how to cultivate holy friendships and build partnerships across diversity. Urban pastoral leaders must have the courage to speak prophetically, and the know-how to work for social change. In the midst of their work, they embody a sabbath spirituality that points others toward the Source of renewal.

The experiences of pastors in our program point to the importance of cultivating practices of sabbath keeping early in the formation for ministry, supporting periodic sabbaticals for pastors throughout their ministries, and developing congregational ecologies that nurture sabbath practices among laity and clergy. We saw how very countercultural the practice of sabbath keeping is, how pastors' identities and understandings of success—and the expectations their congregations place on them—are bound up with productivity and immediate usefulness. In cultivating sabbath practices, we need to resist a utilitarian justification for the practice. Too often pastors described sabbath in instrumental terms, as a tool to increase their effectiveness and efficiency. Practices of sabbath keeping are indeed foundational to ministry. Yet, this is so not because sabbath keeping is a self-help tool or leadership strategy; rather, it is a practice that embodies and renews a right understanding of God as Creator, our own identity as created beings, and the gift of freedom from unceasing work. Sabbath is, I would say, a practice that enables us to participate in God's reconciling, humanizing work in the world.

We have come to believe that field education needs to be situated in congregational teaching sites that explicitly covenant with seminaries to nurture student interns in integrated practices of sabbath keeping, spiritual renewal, study, and friendship. This means that we need to build congregational ecologies to support the practices of pastoral excellence.

At the same time, our work with pastors made clear that our own rhythms as a seminary were out of sync with the rhythms we had invited these pastors to live into: balance of work and rest, community and solitude, giving and self-care. And this seemed to be a problem widespread in theological education. Moreover, given our clear conviction about the importance of place, it became apparent that we needed to go even further in contextualizing our curriculum and pedagogy. We currently are rolling out a new MDiv curriculum that attends seriously to such issues.

Remaining, though, is the challenge of addressing academic formation—how seminary professors are formed in habits and practices, shaped by the expectations of the academy, in ways that may not make us the best models for pastors-in-formation. We need a level of self-reflection that goes beyond project-oriented discussions about the relationship between academy and church. I am convinced that there is a serious discrepancy between the kinds of practices we assert are constitutive of pastoral excellence and the practices in which we are formed as academics. As the School of Theology community interacted with the urban pastors, for example, we noticed that one of the most uncomfortable issues for us was the question of how faculty model balance, self-care, and sabbath practices in our own lives. One pastor posed this challenging question: "Would a covenant among faculty members regarding their own sabbath living help to ensure that we model for the students what we are asking of them?" More than one faculty member called herself "a dreadful example." Seminary faculty are formed in particular contexts—including the academic context that emphasizes rigor, accountability to one's guild, productivity (for example, "publish or perish"), and rhythms of advancement that may conflict with the demands of concurrent life stages (for example, tenure clock competing with biological clock, work competing with family). What notions of time and balance, friendship and self-care result? How then do faculty model practices of pastoral excellence to their students? Like students and pastors, professors need guidance and structural incentives to cultivate practices of sabbath keeping, authentic peer community, and spiritual nurture.

I have been blessed by learning about all the good work of the Engaging Pastors project. As you continue your own reflections, I would leave you with some wondering questions:

- What needs to happen to enable pastors, seminary faculty, and students to read our contexts/communities skillfully and with love, generosity, and delight?

- How might continued work together enable pastors, seminary faculty, and students to read ourselves skillfully and with love, generosity, and delight?

- What are the habits and practices that shape virtues in which pastoral authority (and teaching authority) might be grounded?

- What changes need to occur in the ecologies of our institutions (church and seminary) so that these virtues might be cultivated more fully?

- How is our joy sustained?

Learning one

Both the practice and teaching of ministry are strengthened when pastors and professors regularly engage each other in ways that honor the knowledge and expertise of each.

Reflections on learning one

Dorothy Nickel Friesen

*Both the practice and teaching of ministry are strengthened
when pastors and professors regularly engage each other
in ways that honor the knowledge and expertise of each.*

What does it take to get pastors and professors to engage each other? Evidently the answer is money. Without a huge grant, the question may be asked, would we ever engage each other? As a conference minister who participated in a colloquy, I would have been honored to pay my own way just to be part of the colloquy, but it was a sweet blessing to endorse my honorarium check over to a middle judicatory in exchange for an absence of several days. Little did they know that the check was only a fraction of the satisfaction and joy I received for being a minister of the gospel by serving the church in this way as a conference minister.

Dorothy Nickel Friesen is Conference Minister for Western District Conference of Mennonite Church USA. She helped to develop the original Engaging Pastors grant, participated in a day of working together as conference ministers and faculty in Pittsburgh in 2006, and was part of the Pastor-Faculty Colloquy for Area Church and Conference Ministers in 2007–08. In her role as conference minister, Dorothy especially appreciates the opportunity to shape congregational leadership through pastoral searches and continuing education.

I fell in love again with theological discussion with colleagues who "get it" when it comes to combining scholarship and service; combining the head and heart (although the writer of Hebrews might suggest they are the same); and combining U.S. and Canada, men and women, Anglo and Hispanic, denomination, area conference or church, and pastor—for we are one glorified body of Christ. It is with a sense of thankfulness and a sense of urgency that I reflect on our engagement with each other.

Actually, the word *engage* is a metaphor for preparation for marriage. I wonder, are we engaged, together anticipating the marriage ministry? What is ready to be consummated? And just who are the willing, consenting partners? Well, each metaphor has its limits, and maybe it is fine to anticipate the joy of engagement rather than the reality of marriage!

Observation #1: Surprise!

It was evident to me in both the extensive and very helpful reporting that we were given in preparation for this consultation that both pastors and professors were surprised to discover all kinds of things.

We love our congregations! I am guessing that the work of ministry is always tempered with the overwork of pastoring, so we forget our incredible love for the people of God, or at least fail to articulate how much we enjoy and appreciate the congregation. We were surprised to articulate so easily that most of us truly love our work and our small part in the larger picture of discipleship, faith formation, and experiencing the closeness of the reign of God.

Professors were startled to discover how important they were to pastoral formation. The reality that AMBS grads (in this case) were lifelong friends of fellow students was only matched by recalling the classes, worship in the chapel, spiritual direction, and faith-shaped lectures and prayers that had stayed with them. In short, the person of the professor and the person of the pastor were affecting each other's lives in ways we had not articulated.

We found out how narrow our contexts are. Professors saw how Anglo they were when faced with the seminario in Dallas. What micro-world had they imagined when teaching a routine class in Elkhart? What good was AMBS to an undocumented Hispanic pastor in Dallas? We were surprised, however, at how easily we learned from each other, how thirsty we were for each other's passion for Jesus Christ, how much we looked to the same Bible for guidance, and how much we loved to talk with each other.

We were surprised by each other's loneliness. No one prepared us for those first years in ministry—alone, isolated—with few peers around for discussion. Or how much we missed the classroom, in spite of our grumbling about heavy reading loads, endless reflection papers, and long class periods. No one told professors that they would study by themselves a lot, counsel individual students a lot, and feel that they were teaching in isolation—often convinced that their discipline was the most critical for the students. And most professors were surprised that pastors had not taken their courses because the classes were not required for the MDiv degree.

We were surprised that no structures exist for regular conversation between academy and judicatory. There are no formal exchanges, no structures, and little encouragement to become engaged. We are all wandering students, full of expertise, but we do not find a classroom where we can sit down together.

Observation #2: Just who has authority to lead?

The major theme that crept into nearly every colloquy was the uncomfortable question about leadership. Just what can or may pastors do? Who teaches the Bible? Who leads? Who shapes the missional nature of the congregation? And what difference do professors make in shaping a student's theology of leadership?

Both pastors and professors mused about the relative confusion regarding authority and leadership in the Mennonite church. We have a very egalitarian view of leadership that can also be an entry point for all who sense a call from God to become a leader in the church—be that professor or pastor. However, shaping leaders—actually forming leaders—seems absent at worst and complicated at best. Professors are focused on knowledge and its power, and rightfully so. Pastors are focused on ministry, and rightfully so. However, each is a leadership function, and each must rise to speak out of its unique position.

I am struck that some pastors never teach a Bible study. They have other gifted congregational members—some with advanced degrees—who can offer excellent leadership, and that is good. Some pastors are never asked to create a vision or mission strategy for the congregation. Who designs worship? Who determines the outreach program for the church? What faith formation experiences are expected for children and youth? What curriculum is used for children, youth, and adults? Even within teams of a multi-staffed congregation, it's not clear how pastors will lead. With the talk of gift discernment, we have uncovered some tools for exercising authority, but I submit that this is one area of huge confusion among pastors. I'm guessing that professors have not thought directly about their courses as authority-shaping environments.

Observation #3: Seminary is not sufficient.

I believe that seminary is not sufficient training for pastoring. Don't get me wrong. It is absolutely indispensable, but it is not sufficient. The church has abdicated its role in shaping leaders and does not provide structures to support pastors. Congregations do not see themselves as places of theological discernment. In short, I don't see how this whole pastoring thing works at all!

As a conference minister, I see bright, eager, and good students arrive at the congregation's doorstep, only to be faced with doing all those firsts with total fear and angst: funeral, council meeting, local ministerial meeting, quilting day, potluck, and prayer at the local high school's commencement. Suddenly all the Greek and Hebrew, the mission/peace, the Luke/Acts, the peace and conflict, and the chapel worship just fly away, elusive and ethereal. The overwhelming sense of inadequacy, of naïveté, of a lack of experience, and of loneliness shut down even the most gifted, and they stumble into a traditional role of servant but not of leader. I, as conference minister, listen to tearful stories of failure, inadequacy, wonderment, and bewilderment, or stories of bravado and lone ranger attitudes that are both destructive and unchristian. How did that happen? How did the curriculum that they loved at AMBS seem so distant in the prairies of Kansas or the sprawl of Dallas? How come that professor who inspired us so much is now a distant, nearly mythical character, so far away from my pastor as she stares into her bowl of Cheerios on another Monday morning after a grueling Sunday?

The truth is not that AMBS is a bad seminary. The truth is not that the students are failures. The truth is not that the calling was a hoax. The truth is not the congregation is a bad place.

The truth is that we believed that seminary was enough. The truth is that we thought the congregation would be eager to have us. The truth is that we thought conference ministers would be there for us. The truth is that we didn't even know we had a conference minister.

We must rethink our relationships in the Mennonite church between seminary, congregation, and conference. We must redefine professor, pastor, and conference minister. We must engage each other in thoughtful, deliberate, and critical ways. The Engaging Pastors project proved over and over that what we longed for could be accomplished. Now what?

Observation #4: How shall we honor each other?

I suspect that seminary education is at a crossroads. The model of sending eager men to sit in a cloistered seminary environment and to be called to a Mennonite congregation and live happily ever after is gone. Equally gone are thriving congregations that are naturally inclined to call on AMBS to fill their pulpits. How will we engage this age, this time, this mission?

I wonder sometimes if we need to be better at AMBS (the community-based theological setting) and in the congregation (the practice-based theological center). Could we engage clusters of pastor-peers with professors as a regular practice? Could we, as conference ministers, be invited to be more included in theological reflection centers, offering continuing education seminars and connections between professors and pastors? Could we provide denominational requirements that said all ordinations of active pastors would be reviewed every five years by a team of professors and conference and denominational leaders with a view to continuous improvement? How might professors be invited to judicatory gatherings as a regular feature, so that every year a team of professors meets with a team of conference ministers at the annual conference ministers' meeting? And how about conference ministers being required to have continuing education to remain in their positions? Well, that's a lot to dream about.

Observation #5: We must keep up the momentum.

Mennonites should not let go of this impulse for connecting aspects of leadership in the church. There is so much to gain if we keep up the momentum of current collaboration, and too much to lose if we do not. With Sara Wenger Shenk coming to AMBS, I declare that AMBS and Eastern Mennonite Seminary be one seminary with one president and administer two campuses for the good of the church. It's time to collaborate, not compete. For the sake of the church, it's time to think outside of Elkhart and Harrisonburg as important. Dallas is ready to be a center. I'm guessing Denver could be a center. And certainly Los Angeles and Portland and Minneapolis are ready. Going north of the 49th parallel, we already have other important sites of Mennonite education. But this may be meddling—and so be it.

Conclusion

For the sake of the church, let's engage professor and pastor. For the sake of the God's mission in the world, let's continue not just to talk but to create new ways to call leaders, new ways to form leaders, and new ways to be leaders. It's a surprising time, and we just might be the ones to shape a new generation of Mennonite leaders. In short, let's get married.

Reflections on learning one

Gayle Gerber Koontz

*Both the practice and teaching of ministry are strengthened
when pastors and professors regularly engage each other
in ways that honor the knowledge and expertise of each.*

I would like to begin by briefly explaining the Engaging
Pastors projects in which I participated specifically, so that
you understand the context out of which I am speaking. I
was part of the first Pastor-Faculty Colloquy, which included
pastors from diverse ethnic groups and during which we
talked about practices of the church in light of John Howard
Yoder's *Body Politics*. I participated in a Listening Project
weekend at Cincinnati Mennonite Fellowship, learning about
the church's life and ministry and hearing from its pastor,
a recent AMBS graduate. I was part of a course revision—
Human Sexuality and Christian Ethics—which allowed

Gayle Gerber Koontz is Professor of Theology and Ethics at AMBS. Gayle
helped to develop the Engaging Pastors grant, and she participated in an Engaging Pastors Seminary Course Revision, a Listening Project, and the 2005–06 Pastor-
Faculty Colloquy on the work of John Howard Yoder and pastoral ministry, and
she met with several pastors on sabbatical. Most satisfying in her role as seminary
professor is seeing the many students she has known over the years carry the light
of Christ into the complex and suffering world that God loves so deeply.

a pastor to participate in the course for the semester and involved a consultation meeting with a group of local pastors. In addition, I have interacted with a number of pastors who have been here on sabbatical over the last five years.

From my faculty perspective I think there have been two primary ways Engaging Pastors projects have strengthened my (our) teaching of pastoral ministry:

1. Communicating the diversity and creativity of ecclesial contexts and life

One of my jobs here at AMBS is to teach Theology of the Church, which is both an ecclesiology course and a course in ecumenical formation. While I have visited quite a variety of congregations in several countries during the past twenty-seven years, when I am home (which is most of the time), I attend one congregation. Because the contexts, histories, testimonies, and current struggles of various Mennonite and other congregations are so diverse, it is imperative for my ability to teach well and relevantly to have a broad perspective on the church. This breadth enables me to use concrete illustrations in teaching that demonstrate how context shapes the theological and ethical issues the church grapples with, and the kind of contemporary theology its members embrace. I also draw from the experience of different congregations that have found creative ways to address gender or sexuality issues, for example, or to incorporate children into the life of the congregation.

Both the colloquy and the Listening Project visit provided enough time and space to reflect with pastors and congregational leaders at a level substantive enough to truly learn from them in ways that enriched and helped reshape teaching (for example, discussion of the theology and practice of communion, especially of whether it should be open to unbaptized children and adults). Pastors on sabbatical have also contributed to both formal and informal teaching in this way. Last year a pastoral couple talked about their congregation's extended process of decision making regarding homosexuality. This year a single woman pastor met informally with a group of younger single women, sharing some of the challenges and joys of pastoral ministry given her gender and singleness. Usually pastors on sabbatical will offer some aspect of their work or wisdom in a community forum.

I would value ongoing engagements between congregations and faculty members. Perhaps a congregation from each district could invite a faculty member every few years to visit and learn from them. (I rarely receive invitations from the wider church to visit or engage congregations.) I would value having adequate honoraria funds to be able to regularly invite pastors to join class sessions in the history, theology, and ethics department. I would also value ways for faculty to engage pastors more substantively than saying hi in the hallways during Pastors Week at AMBS, as well as ongoing connections with pastors on sabbatical at AMBS who have gifts to offer us while they abide here.

2. Fostering greater integrity and discernment in curriculum revision

A move toward greater integrity and discernment can happen on a level as simple a level as shifting the emphasis in a particular course. For example, it became clear that the course I teach related to sexuality should give much more attention to pornography because pastors reported that this was the single highest-priority issue in sexual ethics in their congregations. At the same time, curricular revision may occur on a more foundational level. Mennonite conference ministers working on articulating competencies for pastors have been significant conversation partners in formulating MDiv educational goals.

An important area for further discernment is what aspects of education for ministry can best be done at AMBS with the multiple resources (including faculty and peers) available in such a setting, and what can best be done in the early years of ministry. How can seminary and conferences best work together at resourcing learning in both settings? It has been obvious to me for many years that congregations do much teaching of pastors. Indeed, some are forthright in saying they do much more of it than the seminary does, and that is a significant place where we need to do some additional curricular planning. (Some pastors, of course, wish their congregations had more education in what it means to be good congregations.) I would welcome creative thinking about how structures might be put in place so that seminary faculty, pastors, and congregational and conference leaders could connect in an ongoing way to enhance pastor-congregation relationships for the sake of the work of the church in the world.

A few additional comments

Students in the MDiv program have a variety of vocational directions. In addition to congregational pastoral ministry, students have come from or intend to enter mission and service assignments; they expect to teach in church or college settings, work in church agency administrative roles, or serve as chaplains or Christian counselors. The variety of contexts and roles in which MDiv graduates find themselves and for which we must prepare them is more diverse than Engaging Pastors may appear to suggest. Colloquies or other engagements in the future that would connect us with those who are ministering in a wider variety of roles could also be fruitful.

While the opportunities that Engaging Pastors has provided have been rich, it is not the only venue in which faculty engage pastors (not counting our own local ministers and churches we visit because they are home to our extended family and friends). For example, a significant number of the students I have taught over the years come to AMBS with a number of years of pastoral or other church leadership experience already under their belts. Some are currently in pastoral or other ministry assignments. These students also teach me and other students as we explore everything from how we image God to how congregations can relate more provocatively and honestly to their local contexts.

What was unique in my experiences with the Engaging Pastors projects was that some of the pastors I encountered were highly experienced, having completed their education years ago, and therefore were not connecting regularly with AMBS faculty. Several of the pastors, more ethnically diverse, had never visited AMBS, knew almost nothing about it, and would have taken no initiative to connect with us. Without Engaging Pastors there would have not been opportunity to learn from their approaches to pastoral ministry and theological education. Finally, funds were available for us as faculty to travel to ministry settings and experience them firsthand rather than hear about them secondhand. This permitted us to hear voices of congregational leaders other than the pastors, articulating both appreciation for their pastors and narratives of congregational struggles along with encouraging developments over the years.

Reflections on learning one

Samuel Olarewaju

*Both the practice and teaching of ministry are strengthened
when pastors and professors regularly engage each other
in ways that honor the knowledge and expertise of each.*

The thesis of this presentation is that the practice and teaching of ministry are strengthened when pastors and professors regularly engage each other in ways that honor the knowledge and expertise of each. My response to this thesis comes from the vantage point of being at the same time a teacher and a practitioner of ministry. From my experience, there is no doubt that both the teaching and pastoral aspects of my ministry were enhanced as a result of my sabbatical leave last spring at AMBS. I would like to focus more on the benefits of my AMBS experience that relate to my pastoral ministry.

Samuel Olarewaju is Pastor at Berean Fellowship Church in Youngstown, Ohio, a church of Ohio Conference of Mennonite Church USA, and Adjunct Professor at Liberty University in Lynchburg, Virginia. Samuel participated in the Engaging Pastors Pastor Sabbatical program in 2009, staying on campus for several weeks. In his current ministry assignment, Samuel enjoys teaching the Word and applying it to real live issues facing the church.

There are two areas where I would say I was particularly strengthened as a result of my sabbatical leave. The first is that I felt strengthened by the refreshing change of environment that the program provided. Variety is the spice of life, and life in the ministry is no exception. Much of a pastor's duty involves giving to others. There are those who need guidance, those who need biblical knowledge of the truth, those who need to be encouraged, those who need hope and joy in grief, those who need reconciliation in their relationships with God and others, and those who need to be dissuaded from evil. The pastor is constantly bombarded with these and other needs, and for each need he or she is expected to have something appropriate to give. So, a pastor can easily feel drained and empty as he or she is constantly giving to others. The sabbatical leave provided me a much needed opportunity to refill and be refreshed spiritually, emotionally, and intellectually. My members noticed that after my sabbatical, I returned to my pastoral duties with more excitement and vigor to serve the Lord.

A lady called the church office on Monday morning, anxiously wanting to get counsel from her pastor. When told that it was the pastor's day off, she responded, "The Devil doesn't take a day off; why should the pastor?" The secretary wisely and gently replied, "Ma'am, that's why the pastor needs a day off—so he doesn't become like the Devil." Every pastor needs a sabbatical leave to receive, refill, and refresh, in order to be ready to continue the task against the Devil. What better place for a pastor to be refreshed than a place like AMBS, where the human and material resources abound?

The second area where I was strengthened was in the area of knowledge. The questions I had while attending seminary are different from the questions I now have as a pastor. To be sure, some of the answers I received as a student in the seminary were not answers to questions I was asking, if I had any questions at all. The fact is I don't remember any serious ministry-related questions I had back then. Many of the answers I received were answers to questions framed by my professors or by others who had some ministry experience prior to or after their seminary training. Some of those answers were relevant to my pastoral ministry later; some were not or have yet to be relevant. This reminds me of the satirical definition of a theologian as one who is seeking answers to questions no one is asking, such as, how many angels can dance on the head of a pin? This portrayal, of course, is an exaggeration that points to human weakness in the face of the noble task of theology. It is, nevertheless, a salient reminder of the continuous need for us to engage one another to bridge the gap between the seminary and the church.

There is no doubt that many a seminarian, upon graduating, left the seminary armed with answers to questions that few if any were asking in the church—questions like: Is the resurrection body physical or spiritual? Did God elect the saved after decreeing the creation, fall, and redemption, according to sublapsarianism? Or did God elect the saved prior to decreeing the creation, fall, and redemption, according to supralapsarianism? While we do not intend to deny the historical value of some of these questions and answers within Christianity, they should not be overemphasized to the neglect of live questions facing the church in the twenty-first century. Seminary training is not meant to produce graduates ready to address the issues of yesterday while failing to address the questions that the average Christian is asking today.

I still remember the wise counsel I received from one of my teachers when, as a fresh graduate from Bible College, I was considering whether to go straight to seminary or to land a pastoral job. She advised that I get a pastoral job in order to get some ministry experience that would then inform the formulation of my own questions for which I would seek answers later in the seminary.

Many pastors in ministry have post-seminary questions of their own for which they would like to seek answers. I had some questions I wanted to address, but the tyranny of the exigencies of the pastorate did not provide the right atmosphere to address some of my questions. However, the sabbatical at AMBS provided a unique opportunity to seek answers to a couple of the questions I had stored away in my freezer of to-be-answered questions.

In part, the thesis that this presentation is addressing assumes—and rightly so—that there is a mutual benefit for each group when pastors and seminary professors "engage each other in ways that honor the knowledge and expertise of each." This statement is true, and both sides need to promote such interactions. However, I would like to propose that beyond engaging the pastors, the professors also need sabbaticals that take them out of the ivory tower of the seminaries to engage the laity directly and get a firsthand experience of the state of the church today. Just as pastors need periodically to go back to the seminaries to find answers to the live questions facing them, professors need to go into the trenches and spend some time in the shoes of the pastors, testing the principles and theories formulated in the seminaries. The fallout of a seminary professor's engagement with a given pastor is a vicarious experience of the pastorate through the eyes of that particular pastor. By engaging the laity directly during a one-month sabbatical in the church, for instance, a professor would have a direct experience of the church's life from his or her own perspective from the pulpit.

We have a nomadic group in Nigeria that does not put much practical value on vicarious experience. When members of this group visit a doctor for treatment, they assess the effectiveness of any prescription given to them by asking the doctor whether he or she has had the same ailment before and whether the same medication was used by the doctor effectively. When I was in the seminary as a student, one of my theology professors went on a summer mission trip overseas. Upon his return and until many of us graduated, there was a noticeable difference for the better in that professor's ministry on the campus. The curriculum did not change, but the professor's perspective on the ministry for which he was training others and his relationship with his students changed. That is what this is all about—engaging each other to effect a change for the better in all of us as we serve the Lord.

Report on learning one

Listening Committee

Both the practice and teaching of ministry are strengthened when pastors and professors regularly engage each other in ways that honor the knowledge and expertise of each.

Resonance with learning one

- Across the board there was strong affirmation of learning one.

Emerging themes

- Middle judicatory is a vital link in the ecology of ministry; area church and conference ministers need to help bridge the gap between pastors and professors.
- The first five years of ministry are critical for continued formation and learning.
- We need substantive, ongoing support: mentors, etc.

Significant questions

- Who gives leadership to the ecology of ministry?

- How is trust generated and sustained in the ecology of ministry?

- Who finances the ecology of ministry and the engagement needed to make it happen?

- Define more carefully the role of each part of the ecology of ministry. How can we be most effective?

- How can we think more comprehensively about coordinating the ecology of ministry?

- How do pastors and professors honor each other? Does the learning statement imply that we have not honored each other in our past engagement?

- How do we take seriously the undercurrents of stress related to cultural diversity, geographical distance, etc.?

Trajectories and suggestions

- This learning identifies an agenda for the broader church structure (area churches and conferences, denominations, agencies).

- We need to make better stewardship use of the forums where we already gather.

- Defining competencies and authorizing credentialing may be a critical intersection where the entire ecology of ministry is engaged or could better be engaged.

- We need to strengthen continuing education and recredentialing of pastors from other denominations.

Musings by the Listening Committee

- Will the idea of ecology of ministry last?
- The absence of the denomination in the learning is evident, and it came through clearly in the responses.

Learning two

There is an urgent need and opportunity for pastoral, biblical, and teaching authority to be strengthened in the Mennonite church.

Reflections on learning two

Mary Schertz

There is an urgent need and opportunity
for pastoral, biblical, and teaching authority
to be strengthened in the Mennonite church.

The small girl was not a particularly charming child. She
was awkward, scattered, and had a penchant to chatter.
But it was Christmas Eve in the small country church, and
most of us dredged up some tolerance as Elizabeth marched
up to the front of the church with her violin. Ignoring
everyone, she stood there with her child-sized violin under
her chin and her bow hand down at her side. The moment
stretched . . . and grew some more. Absolutely still, tiny
Elizabeth gathered her forces, her concentration fierce. All
rustling ceased. We, too, finally were still. Then, she drew
her bow and played the simple melody beautifully—not

Mary Schertz is Professor of New Testament and Director of the Institute of
Mennonite Studies at AMBS. Mary helped to develop the Engaging Pastors grant
and serves on the Engaging Pastors Oversight Committee. She participated in three
Engaging Pastors Course Revisions, a Listening Project, and the 2006–07 Pastor-Fac-
ulty Colloquy on Pastor as Teacher of the Bible in the Congregation. She also led two
Pastor-Faculty Study Groups and met with pastors on sabbatical.

perfectly, but lyrically, with haunting sweetness. She made us forget our adult tolerance. She made us forget how small she was. She made us attend not to her, nor to ourselves, but to the music. It was a compelling, authoritative performance— one I yet remember.

> There is an urgent need and opportunity for pastoral, biblical, and teaching authority to be strengthened in the Mennonite church.

There is, of course, some distance between Elizabeth's Christmas Eve solo and the issues of pastoral, biblical, and teaching authority in the Mennonite church. Nevertheless, I think we can learn some things from her. Elizabeth teaches us that authority is both given and taken. She teaches us that authority is both talent and training. Most importantly, the small violinist teaches us that authority ultimately serves neither the people nor the performer but the aesthetics of being and the Giver of that being.

Authority is given and taken.

The small country congregation of which Elizabeth was a part gave her time and space to lead them. That is probably not how the planners of the service thought about her role in the program, but that is in fact what it was. Elizabeth, however, also took authority in ways most small children playing their instruments in Christmas Eve services do not. She took herself and the gift she had to offer seriously, and in that seriousness required us to take her and her offering seriously, as well. Her poise and her devotion to the music simply gave no quarter to the condescension with which we were prepared to listen.

Pastoral, biblical, and teaching authority are likewise both given and taken. Congregations and conferences bestow authority on pastors when they call, license, and ordain them. We give the Bible authority in our liturgy, discernment, and devotions. Educational institutions give teachers authority when they employ them, and students give teachers authority when they take their classes.

Our beloved denomination is hugely ambivalent about how, when, and why we confer authority in each of these areas. Some congregations call pastors and give them a job description but withhold, relationally or structurally, the authority they need to fulfill their responsibilities. There is little that is more debilitating to pastors. Such crippling may happen more often to associate pastors than to lead pastors and more often to female pastors than to male pastors. But it happens too frequently, and it is too big a waste. We are ambivalent about the Bible as authority for living Christianly. We fail to read it, or we read it badly, shoring up our own untruths. We claim that the Bible needs to speak with one coherent voice, and we overlook contradictions and minority voices. Or we claim that the Bible speaks in as many voices as there are readers and interpreters.

We are ambivalent about the authority we confer on our teachers. Sometimes we give them too much authority, hanging on their every word as if they could speak no wrong. Sometimes we give them too little authority, denigrating what they do as unnecessary or elitist. Sometimes we expect them to do for us what we ought to be doing for ourselves.

I suspect that some ambivalence about authority will always be part of who we are as Mennonites, and maybe a certain amount of skepticism is good. The amount and kind of ambivalence is, however, hindering the mission of God in the world and, I think, making us unhappy. For both God's sake and our own, we need to work at these issues.

The matter does not lie solely in the conferring of authority. I fear we are also training leaders who are reluctant to take authority—and for good reason, given our ambivalence.

Taking one's authority, one's proper, humble, and conferred authority, however, is too important to a healthy faithfulness to the mission of God to allow our denominational ambivalence to derail us—though shy we may be. Nevertheless, in our training of pastors, biblical interpreters, and teachers, we must talk about, practice, and support leaders living into their authority. Waiting to work at the issues of taking authority until we have solved our ambivalence about giving authority would let us off the hook here at AMBS. It would let us off the hook as conference ministers. It would let us off the hook as pastors.

But I do not think we can wait. Furthermore, I have a hunch that our ambivalence about giving authority and our reluctance to take authority cannot be solved in isolation. We have to work at both together. The authority we gave small Elizabeth was ambivalent at best. She took it and ran with it—and we were all transported.

Authority depends on talent and training.

Our tiny violinist had native talent. That was clear. Some of us could not have played as musically as she did—at any age or after any amount of training. Authority in pastoral leadership, biblical interpretation, and teaching also depends on talent. We likely have not recognized that reality sufficiently. Notions, valid and not so valid, about the priesthood of all believers, coupled with our pervasive ambivalence about authority and leadership, have contributed to a harmful—if democratic—conviction that anyone can be a pastor, interpret the Bible, or teach. Certainly there are ways any believer can and should participate in ministry, Bible reading, and biblical discernment, as well as Christian education. But let us not confuse healthy, appropriate, vigorous participation with the kind of talent that we develop and in which we invest authority. Leadership in all the areas we are considering takes spiritual gifts of wisdom, maturity, intelligence, imagination, patience, perseverance, humor, and humility, among others. Not every believer has these gifts in sufficient quantity or quality to lead. Our communal humility on this point has dangerously approached a communal arrogance. We have been so reluctant to elevate any one of us that we have unwittingly and unhelpfully elevated all of us. We cannot all be pastors, biblical interpreters, and teachers. We are not all so called.

Our tiny violinist did not just have talent. She was trained. I do not know the particulars, but whatever her training, Elizabeth had become a disciplined player. She had not only learned the technique and the melody; she had learned to respect the art and her talent. She had learned what performance demanded and what it gave. Her authority was in part the result of her training.

We must not only discern native talent for leadership but we must together, as congregations, conferences, and seminaries, train leaders in the disciplined practices of pastoral leadership, biblical interpretation, and teaching. If the Engaging Pastors program has taught us anything, it has taught us that each of those components—congregations, conferences and seminaries—has a vital role to perform in the development of leaders. None of us can do that important job on our own. This task seems clear—to define those roles, to respect those roles, and to implement those roles. Congregations cannot afford to dismiss conferences as unnecessary and seminaries as elite. Conferences cannot overlook the vital role congregations play in making pastors, nor can they be content to work in parallel to the seminaries rather than with the seminaries. Seminaries must acknowledge that pastors, biblical interpreters, and teachers learn some of what they need to know on the job. Seminaries must acknowledge as partners both congregations and conferences. Congregations, conferences, and seminaries must all acknowledge and accept themselves as teaching institutions. Neither our suspicions about training nor our defensiveness about training has served us well.

Authority serves the moment and the Giver.

I do not know why small Elizabeth was asked to play or why she gave assent. I suspect that everyone had some notion of serving one another. Elizabeth would fill a slot on the Christmas Eve program and gain some much-needed positive attention. The congregation would feel good about nurturing its children.

All those worthy intentions, however, gave way to the power of the moment and the power of the music itself to call us toward the One who created us all. We were transported. All the kinds of service that we intended happened. Elizabeth served us and we served Elizabeth. But something much more happened. Elizabeth, in serving her gift, served her Creator—whatever her consciousness of this service at the time. In allowing ourselves to be drawn into her music, we also served her gift; but more than that, we served the God who had called us together, given us one another, given us the Bible, and given us Jesus, whose incarnation we were, after all, celebrating. The giving and taking of authority and the talent and training from which the authority grew were ultimately all given over to the moment and the great Giver of that moment.

That, perhaps, is the most critical perspective to gather into ourselves regarding all these issues of leadership and authority. Perhaps traditional hierarchical authority has not so much failed as failed to keep in mind that authority does not ultimately serve those who lead. Perhaps our own foray into servant leadership has not so much failed as failed to keep in mind that authority does not ultimately serve those who are led. Leadership of any kind does not first serve the church. Leadership of any kind first serves the One who created us and called us to be the body of Christ, the Christ whose advent awaits us ever new. It is in that spirit, and only in that spirit, that leadership serves the church.

Reflections on learning two

Tim Kuepfer

*There is an urgent need and opportunity
for pastoral, biblical, and teaching authority
to be strengthened in the Mennonite church.*

It's an enormous subject, of course, this learning we have been given to reflect on in this Engaging Pastors project. I've been learning, over the past half-dozen years as pastor at Peace Mennonite Church, that when faced with a huge subject, it's usually wise not to take too ambitious a bite into it. So, as a way to narrow my own response to this thesis, I've chosen to reflect on the idea that *pastoral, biblical, and teaching authority is rooted in the spiritual authenticity of the leader.*

I am sure that the local congregation, our conferences, and schools such as AMBS bear much responsibility for granting,

Tim Kuepfer is Lead Pastor of Peace Mennonite Church in Richmond, British Columbia. He has been involved in Engaging Pastors through the 2006–07 Pastor-Faculty Colloquy on Pastor as Teacher of the Bible in the Congregation, and in the 2005 Clarifying the Call event for pastors in their early years of ministry. Tim especially enjoys the intercultural ministry and friendships that are developing at Peace. He loves the different ethnic foods and reading the Bible together with sisters and brothers from Korea, Sri Lanka, Taiwan, Brazil, China, Hong Kong, and Malaysia. He finds great joy in seeing those who knew nothing about Jesus become disciples.

developing, nurturing, affirming, and limiting the authority of the pastor, but let me attempt my own way into this theme by addressing the leader (myself).

I grew up in a small Amish Mennonite (Beachy Amish) congregation in which the local church leadership was accorded a high level of pastoral, biblical, and teaching authority. The ministers (as we referred to them) were (as I remember them) men (yes, men) of spiritual integrity who led and guided us by their lives of exemplary Christian faithfulness, humility, prayer, discipline, scripture memory, and biblical teaching.

Formal biblical training for our leaders was eschewed—no, spurned—mostly out of concern, I suppose, that "higher learning" would foster pride. What was highly prized among us, however, was our ministers' heart-centred (as opposed to head-centred) commitment to God's Word—both the daily, personal ingesting of scripture and then the regular proclamation of it for the edification of the church. Under the direction of our church leaders, we prayed together a great deal as a congregation, particularly in our Wednesday evening prayer meetings during which we knelt in our pews for long stretches of intercession.

Sermons were the heart of the Sunday morning and Sunday evening services as well as the semi-annual week-long revival meetings and Bible conferences. We were a people formed by scripture and by prayer. Both were provided for us by our spiritual leaders. These leaders were called from within the congregation and set apart ("sanctified!") in their ordination—set apart for the sacred trust of proclaiming the Word to us week in and week out. We actually talked about sanctification (being "set apart") a lot! All the ministers that I can remember accepted this sacred call, this setting apart for the pastoral role, with great seriousness.

It seems to me that the community in which I was reared had, at least in this particular way, a healthier understanding and grounding in this whole matter of pastoral, biblical, and teaching authority than we do in our Mennonite church. Sure, the simple pietistic bent of my upbringing seems to us a bit naive and unsophisticated. I don't doubt it was. I'm not advocating a sort of romantic return to my roots. What I do wonder, however, is whether we've adequately emphasized spiritual formation and (here's that old-fashioned word again) sanctification, in the training, equipping, and calling of pastors.

I've sometimes wondered: Could it be possible that we leaders in the Mennonite church might be (or might once have been) subtly motivated by a bit of an inferiority complex as we've tried to catch up to the rest of the Christian world in our theological higher education? And could not this sort of motivation tempt us, the theologically trained, into a patronizing sort of sophistry? Surely this is not at all the way we would want to be set apart from the untrained and uneducated.

The church of my heritage set apart (sanctified) their leaders with the expectation that they would indeed be set apart in exemplary holiness, faithfulness, and love. Yet, they were not set apart in their daily workaday lives; all our ministers continued to work in their original vocations to support themselves and their families. The upside of this tradition of nonsalaried church leadership was that we expected our leaders to practise a sort of ordinary, everyday holiness. The obvious downside was that, with so little time to prepare sermons, the preaching tended to be repetitive (many might even say trite).

I am grateful for the theological training that I have received. I deeply value my education in the original languages of the scriptures, as well as in historical, biblical, and systematic theology. But I am also grateful for the broad, life-encompassing education I received throughout my childhood, teenage, and young-adult years in my Amish Mennonite church. This spiritual formation was accomplished in an informal partnership of church and home within a rural context where our church was at the centre of all social and ecclesial activities.

My present urban context makes it much more difficult for the church to be so deeply involved in this holistic, life-encompassing spiritual formation in holiness. Is this not the central pastoral challenge: to teach and equip, to practise and pray and model daily discipleship, daily holiness, and daily passion simply to follow Jesus?

We Mennonites are a practical people. We like practical solutions. It seems to me, however, that strengthening the authority of leadership in the Mennonite church will require more than a new set of practical solutions. As I look at my own pastoral ministry over the past six years, I see how intimately connected to leadership authority is the renovation of the heart.

I wonder, then, whether the biblical call to holiness is not central to our concern about leadership authority. In one of his many compelling acts of spiritual leadership and authority, Jesus prays over us what has come to be known as the "high priestly prayer." At the centre of his prayer, Jesus says, "Sanctify them by the truth; your word is truth. . . . For them I sanctify myself, that they too may be truly sanctified" (John 17:17, 19; NIV).

Sanctification and holiness cannot simply be about being more moral or more pure or more righteous. Jesus was already all of that, and yet he says that he has sanctified himself for us. What Jesus has done is set himself apart for our own holiness, that we too might be sanctified (set apart). In a holy fixation, Jesus has put all his energy, all his resources—his whole life—at our disposal, that we too, like him, might be sanctified. What would it mean for us leaders to be sanctified—set apart—for our congregations, as Jesus is set apart for us?

Who among us pastors would not like Hebrews 12:2 to be our epitaph: "She/he had eyes fixed on Jesus." If our congregations are confident in their pastors' spiritual authenticity, will they be reticent to grant appropriate leadership authority? Our churches really should expect their shepherds to be authentically Christ-focussed and Christ-fixated in life and ministry.

Indeed, most of us pastors already struggle far too much with guilt. I, for one, like to comfort myself in the knowledge that I'm not alone in my grappling with the pressures and temptations that pull me into distraction, fragmentation, and even disintegration of pastoral focus, purpose, and priority. Who of us does not want to be set apart, sanctified, centred, focussed? Who would not be thrilled to have their lives and vocations channelled by a singular fixation, a "magnificent obsession," a holy passion for the one thing (one person)?

For our communion invitation, I keep returning to Jesus' words to us, "Come to me, all you that are weary and are carrying heavy burdens, and I will give you rest. Take my yoke upon you, and learn from me, for I am gentle and humble in heart" (Matt. 11:28–29; NRSV). I especially need to hear these words. What if we were to actually do that, be that? And then, what if we—with the same sort of integrity, humility, and authenticity—were able say the same thing? "Come to me!" And what if they really did want to come? What if they trusted us enough to come, follow, learn, rest, be? It's enormously comforting to know that Jesus' holy obsession is our sanctification.

What might it look like for us to accept Jesus' yoke? What would it take for us to be able to say with confidence those words that the apostle Paul was so fond of saying: "Imitate me!" "Follow me, as I follow Christ" (1 Cor. 4:16, 11:1; Phil 3:17; 1 Thess. 1:6; 2 Thess. 3:7, 9)?

What, then, does spiritual formation look like in our congregations, in our conferences, and right here at AMBS? What could it look like in our classes, in our monthly pastors' gatherings, in our premarital counselling sessions, or in our worship committee meetings? How shall we lead with authority in the middle of it all?

Who is responsible for the tone, the vibe, the undercurrents, the ethos, the spiritual temperature, and the culture of the institutions into which we are called? Is it not we who are called, authorized, and set apart—sanctified—for leadership?

What is it about AMBS, or Peace Mennonite Church, or Mennonite Church Canada that makes this a sanctified community, a holy place? Could we, could I, could you begin to respond to that question in a way that is specific, intentional, focussed, and holy?

May God grant us so to live.

Reflections on learning two

Jerry Buhler

There is an urgent need and opportunity
for pastoral, biblical, and teaching authority
to be strengthened in the Mennonite church.

As I scan the directory of pastors and congregations in my area church, I am inspired and immensely grateful. I know that very fine pastoral leadership is happening. I know that intense hours are being spent crafting biblically sound sermons. I know that lonely people are being visited, small people are being noticed, and subdued voices are being heard. I know that people are being nurtured into baptism, blessed in their relationships, and given a farewell of hope when they die. I see this, and I hear of this.

Jerry Buhler is Area Church Minister for Mennonite Church Saskatchewan. He participated in an Engaging Pastors–sponsored day of working together as conference ministers and faculty in Pittsburgh in 2006 as well as in the Pastor-Faculty Colloquy for Area Church and Conference Ministers in 2007–08. In his role as area church minister, Jerry appreciates the many occasions to celebrate. He treasures the honor of accompanying a congregation through the journey of saying farewell to a pastor, enjoying a valuable interim season, searching for a new pastor, and finally celebrating the promise of a new partnership.

While all this goodness dominates, I also hear the exasperated voices that lament the sometimes low level of biblical literacy and the voices that bemoan seeming ambivalence toward pastoral leadership. I see and hear of this, too.

Still, existing side by side with the illiteracy is a desire for a deeper understanding of scripture. And living alongside the ambivalence is a longing to be led. I hear reports of sparkling adult Sunday school classes with high attendance and intense discussions. I observe congregants who look to their pastors for meaningful direction and take their counsel seriously.

Clearly there is strong acknowledgement among church leaders and seminary leaders that pastoral authority needs to be strengthened, and there is momentum on the part of these leaders to continue moving in that direction. The Engaging Pastors programs have very much affirmed that. This acknowledgement and momentum must be shared by congregations. It is present in congregations here and there, to various degrees and in various forms. It is crucial, however, that congregations become much more united and intentional about calling for and allowing authority and leadership.

Perhaps one of the greatest obstacles to the deepening and strengthening of pastoral authority in churches is the reluctance and/or the inability on the part of congregations to entrust and empower their pastors, to give their pastors a sense of freedom, to give some strength and sway to their pastors' leadership.

While it is understandable that the level of concern about authority and the consequent commitment to its pursuit may not be as deep in the congregation as it is among leadership, the concern and commitment needs to be deepened in order to lessen this disconnect and boost the possibility of leadership becoming a shared force.

Authority is a gift that is given. We recognize it in community. We give it to those among us whom we trust. We share it, we treat it gently, we treat it respectfully. When our ecclesiology is clear and when we have the cohesiveness of knowing what our vocation is as the church, then we are able to pass this gift of authority on to those who we see are called to carry it. There is a kind of letting go that must happen, an enabling that liberates the pastor to lead. Congregations must learn to be diligent in this process and demonstrate a genuine wish to be led.

The pastor must also demonstrate authenticity. The nature of our culture just now is such that authenticity is a stabilizing anchor that many reach for. An authentic pastor is one who will be such a stabilizer by loving the church and being a model of servanthood.

In comparison to the styles of leadership that were prevalent in the first half of the twentieth century, the recent emergence of leadership that carries integrity and influence but is not authoritarian has made it easier for the church to embrace authority. Increased sensitivity to issues of justice and equality in recent decades has also enhanced the integrity of authority and made it generally more welcome. The aversion to authority that paved the way to a poor understanding and implementation of "servant leadership" disappears in the presence of authentic authority.

The increased weight placed on authority in recent years might be recognizable in part as a response to the perceived failure of attempts at servant leadership. A critical question is whether servant leadership was ever given a fair test. The combination of leaders committed to models of servant leadership and congregations containing power-seeking individuals was likely not an uncommon scenario in and around the 1970s.

It is interesting to note the current shift in how pastors regard ordination, a pastoral title, and their explicit identification as a leader. While earlier pastors often avoided ordination and played down their role as leaders, young and newly trained pastors demonstrate a delightful embrace of these.

As always, there is potential for a pendulum-type phenomenon. The regrettable injury that pastors have sometimes experienced has brought a much needed awareness of the importance of boundaries and self-care. With this comes the potential danger of adopting defensive policies that could lead to the repression of rich and happy relationships between pastors and congregations. The authentic pastor will practice self-care rather than self-preservation, subscribe to healthy boundaries rather than entitlement, and model a generosity of service that grows out of a mutual exchange of gifts with the congregation.

Arnold Snyder describes Gelassenheit as "a surrender of control."[1] He writes, "A community of people who are yielded to the living Spirit of God will, ideally, find their way through issues of power and authority in a spirit of prayer, humility, openness, and flexibility."[2] While this ideal has not

---

1. C. Arnold Snyder, "*Gelassenheit* and Power: Some Historical Reflections," *Vision: A Journal for Church and Theology* 5, no. 2 (Fall 2004): 8.

2. Ibid., 12.

always been the reality in the history of Anabaptism, it remains a relevant goal. There is comfort and safety in knowing that authority is a communal pursuit; it does not rest on one individual but is owned together.

There is comfort and relief in knowing that authority and leadership in any given congregation will also be spread and extended over the lifetime of that congregation. No one leader shoulders the entire weight of responsibility for a congregation's life. It is important to maintain realistic, balanced, and healthy expectations, realizing that each of us may only contribute a small sliver of leadership and administer a small dose of authority in a lifetime. How immobilized indeed a conference full of Moseses would be!

This need for pastoral leadership has long been articulated by church leaders and by seminary professors, and more recently, these two groups have engaged in meaningful collaboration to address it. In the colloquy that I was part of, I saw professors and conference ministers model shared authority. The professors expressed an honest interest in the work of conference ministers and how the formation of leaders could be complemented and strengthened. The conference ministers also sent the clear message that they value the academic contribution made by the professors. Working together toward a common list of competencies and outcomes helped us to identify possibilities to explore together in the future.

Congregations need to catch up with this development and enter this collaboration. They need to acquire more confidence in the schools that offer formation and in the conference leadership that offers placement and support. From this confidence will come a heightened eagerness to share the gift of authority.

I believe that the urgency and the opportunity to strengthen authority are alive together in our church and increasingly call us to learn how to dance with them both. It is my hope that the day is coming in the Mennonite church when we will celebrate authority, when we will be lifted by it—not to places where selected egos are satisfied, but to places where good news is heard, sight is recovered, release is proclaimed, and oppression lifted. To our blinking surprise, we will see that we have been given authority because we obediently tied towels around our waists and knelt at each other's feet.

Report on learning two

Listening Committee

*There is an urgent need and opportunity
for pastoral, biblical, and teaching authority
to be strengthened in the Mennonite church.*

Resonance with learning two

After yesterday's fairly straightforward, "Should it happen? Yes, and here's how," this day's learning took us to the land where the wild things are. There was much less consensus, with more nuanced support and some disagreement.

- The wording of the learning itself is unclear, so there is a lot of ambiguity about what is being asserted here.

- There is a lot of ambivalence about the notion of authority itself.

- When asked whether this learning rings true, groups offered a variety of responses:

  ○ It is not true for all congregations. Or, it is true in ways that must be nuanced by the context and culture of the congregation.

◦ Yes, it is true, but:

> It depends on authority being rightly understood and practiced.

> It depends on trust levels.

> It depends on congregational culture; authority is different in dominant Anglo Mennonite congregations than in other racial/ethnic congregations.

> It must be invitational.

> It is less clear for new pastors.

◦ There were some solid yesses. It is not only true but urgent.

◦ Other groups felt that it may not be urgent.

◦ One group suggested that what is urgent is that we don't have a common understanding of authority and the multiple dimensions of authority. Others said that there is an urgency to empower leaders among the laity. Urgency was confirmed, but it is a complex matter.

• Engagement with this particular learning has the most potential for substantive change. The other learnings relate to structural change, but this goes to the heart of the matter.

• Could this be a kairos moment in Mennonite Church USA? (Whether or not Mennonite Church Canada needs a kairos moment was left unsaid.)

• The learning assumes that ambivalence is bad, but perhaps it can be seen as a blessing.

- The key learning lacks clarity related to biblical, pastoral, and teaching authority.

Emerging themes

- Not only is the wording of the learning unclear, but the notion of authority itself is unclear. We need more clarity about what authority means (what it authorizes one to do, to say, to be) and what it does not mean (what it does *not* authorize). In other words: What are the limits of authority so that it doesn't become its perversion—authoritarianism? The implication we read between the lines: It could be dangerous to set about on an urgent project of strengthening authority if we cannot yet very clearly and concretely name what it is and what it is not.

- However we come to understand the meaning of authority in the church, it needs to be situated within a more comprehensive ecclesiology and our understanding of the priesthood of all believers. We encountered a number of interesting comments on the priesthood, and it seems we desire more work, more conversation—and perhaps more integration—on this point.

- Several groups noted a broader, more general erosion of authority in our surrounding cultures that complicates the entire project and perhaps calls into question its goal.

- Several groups challenged us to share more broadly—as *two* denominations—in crafting *and* implementing expectations and competencies for ministers and therefore to share more broadly in the entire process of credentialing. As mentioned before, however, this can only be done with a great sensitivity to widely varied contexts. Might we strike a balance between the universal and the particular in this project that will aid us in our shared *and* our contextualized understandings of authority?

Significant questions

- How do the learnings from the Engaging Pastors project intersect with the larger Mennonite Church USA conversations about structures of agencies and boards?

- How do we ramp up our efforts toward interdependence across the ecology of ministry?

- How do we read the Bible well, and to whom do we look to tell us that we've read it well? Who can take the authority and make it so?

- Is there interest in Anabaptist models of leadership in our congregations, or are we assuming that?

- Have our diverse histories affected how we view authority?

- Is there a gender dynamic that needs to be identified? Are we willing to give the same level of authority to women as to men?

- How do we hear the congregations in this discussion?

- Who or what determines what constitutes a good reading? Good Mennonites? Good decisions?

- If baptized believers exercised their authority in a healthier way, would that not help us relate better to pastoral authority?

- Is decentralized polity for credentialing a problem or a blessing?

Trajectories and suggestions

- Teaching is needed about leadership and authority.
- We have understood the idea of shepherd as pastoral, when originally it was related to kingship—up-front, authoritative leadership.
- Conference and area church ministers should work clearly with search committees and relate this search to competencies.
- We can have expectations, but that doesn't address authority.

Musings by the Listening Committee

- We have identified disconnects across the learnings: pastors and professors, pastor and community, church and context.
- Are we facing polarities that need to be managed—rather than problems that need to be resolved?
- Is the lack of clarity in the learning itself partly related to the desire for congregational autonomy, and is it a way to sidestep conflict? Has the ambiguity and ambivalence been exaggerated because of the lack of clarity in the way the learning is worded? Was there an intention to be vague, given that clarity would have incited conflict?

- This learning addresses the heart and the core of what pastoral ministry is about; this is an important conversation to be facilitated.

- The scope of the fix on this learning is huge (biblical illiteracy, shrinking numbers, less commitment to faith, lack of confidence in the church, fragmentation, individualization). Does the appeal to authority really fix what we're facing?

Learning three

*The church and the seminary
need to equip pastors and professors
to read and engage their missional contexts
with joy.*

Reflections on learning three

Joel Miller

The church and the seminary need to equip pastors and professors to read and engage their missional contexts with joy.

We've been asked to reflect on the following learning theme: The church and the seminary need to equip pastors and professors to read and engage their missional contexts with joy. I want to set up what I have to say by looking at a scene from Luke's Gospel that offers a window into this process of reading and engaging contexts. It also has some personal significance, as it connects back to my seminary studies. The scene comes from Luke 19, that part of the Gospel after Jesus has already "set his face toward Jerusalem" and is now in the final stage of that journey. When we meet up with him here, he is just on the outskirts of the city, perhaps right

---

Joel Miller is Pastor of Cincinnati Mennonite Fellowship in Cincinnati, Ohio. He was involved in the Engaging Pastors Pastor-Faculty Colloquy for pastors in their early years of ministry in 2008–09 and hosted a Listening Project visit in 2009. Joel greatly enjoys the variety of tasks involved in being a solo pastor, including sermon study and delivery, and walking with people through the sacred moments of life.

at the perch of the Mount of Olives, able to look out over the entire cityscape (most likely still mounted on the colt that has served as the sole float for the day's parade). In verses 41–42 of that chapter, we read this: "As he came near and saw the city, he wept over it, saying, 'If you, even you, had only recognized on this day the things that make for peace! But now they are hidden from your eyes'" (NRSV).

This picture came to life for me during one of the seminary classes I took through the SCUPE program in Chicago. SCUPE stands for the Seminary Consortium for Urban Pastoral Education, and one of the courses involved visiting various ministry sites in the city. During one visit we stopped in on the oldest congregation in the city, the First United Methodist Church at the Chicago Temple, and had the opportunity to meet their staff, hear about their ministries, and tour their historic building. One of the things that caught my eye in the sanctuary was a large wooden relief carving of this scene of Jesus looking out over the city of Jerusalem—with the back of Jesus in the foreground and the city in the background, so the viewer has the experience of seeing Jesus looking out over Jerusalem, or looking with Jesus, over his shoulder, at what Jesus is seeing when he looks out on his beloved city. It was a powerful image, but what made it all the more powerful and provided new insight for me was what occurred when we walked up to a small chapel on the top floor of the church. In the chapel was a similar wooden relief carving, only this time, the city Jesus was looking over was Chicago.

I'd like to offer the observation that what is taking place in this Gospel scene is the very act to which this theme speaks: reading and engaging contexts. What all Jesus saw here—theologically, sociologically, economically, political-ly—could be the subject of another whole symposium. Much of this is what is being worked out in the chapters of Luke that follow, in the events of Holy Week as Jesus engages all of these dynamics within Jerusalem, especially as they pertain to the temple system. What I would like to highlight from this scene as being of particular importance for us is this act of seeing—reading and engaging—and that it was done with such depth of feeling, such pathos, that it caused Jesus to weep. For Jesus, it meant being attentive to the fullness of the time and place into which he was entering. As he prepared to enter into this city, the beloved city of his people, there was an intentional pause, a deep gazing into the reality in front of him. I suggest that this moment of intentional pause for Je-sus—the image on the wood relief—can be a helpful guide as we consider what it means for the church and the seminary to equip pastors and professors to read and engage their mis-sional contexts with joy.

In Cincinnati, where I pastor, there is plenty of reading and engaging to do. I have come to think of our local mis-sional setting as being composed of three different circles to consider. The first circle is our host neighborhood, known as Oakley—the area around the church building, where our neighbors live and work and where my wife Abbie and I have chosen to live with our kids. The second circle is the metro-politan area of Cincinnati and all the interlocking realities within it. I consider the congregation itself to be a third circle, containing its own unique dynamics as we interact with the various neighborhoods and vocational settings in which we find ourselves. Each of these circles deserves its own careful, in-depth, and ongoing reading to enable us to listen for God, to listen to the strengths present in the community, and to listen for particular needs that may exist.

I was able to participate in the 2008–2009 Engaging Pastors Pastor-Faculty Colloquy and found it to be a rich time of reflection with peers about the first years of our ministries. I have read with some interest these summaries of the Engaging Pastors experience over the last number of years. It's my understanding that we carry a common desire to grow in our abilities to be missional leaders. The theology is there, the desire is there, and it's a matter of developing skills and practices, and learning from one another how best to do this.

One of the parts of my schooling at AMBS for which I am most grateful is that I was taught to be a careful, respectful reader of the biblical text. I was given tools of language and hermeneutical frameworks, an introduction to the wealth of study resources available, and tools of parsing, charting, and color-coding texts in a way that helped me internalize the structure and cadence of narrative and poetry. Reading the Bible was modeled for me by professors who have dedicated their lives to the joy of discipline and discovery that comes with this effort. This process helped form in me a sense of joy and confidence in reading scripture. The Bible is a place through which I have been led by skilled guides and where I have the tools I need to continue to explore. It's my turf. Not just my turf, of course, but turf where I feel at home in the community of faith.

But when I compare my sense of being at home in the biblical text with my sense of how I feel in my missional context, there is a large gap that I am still working hard to bridge. If our skills of reading and engaging the text of scripture and the text of the missional setting are the same skill set, which I think they are, then why do I feel so at home reading the Bible but uncertain of my place at our neighborhood community council meeting? If God's mission extends into all aspects of the human community, all facets of creation, then why do I feel hesitant, at times disoriented—like I'm on someone else's turf—when I step into the social service agency, the jail, the downtown high-rise, the courthouse, or the city hall building? I have the ideal of being a congregational leader as well as a community leader, but when I get right down to it, the congregation feels like a much safer, much more familiar place to be. Even if I learn how to parse and diagram the missional setting, familiarizing myself with resources for study and coming to know the languages spoken in these many spheres, I have much to learn, as a missional leader in the church, in terms of how best to engage such a context.

I wonder if other pastors and I, just as we have benefited from skilled tour guides who have taught us to read the biblical text, would also benefit from skilled tour guides who continually teach us how to read the missional setting. Along with visiting and reading Genesis, Isaiah, Luke, and Revelation, I wonder what would happen if we were to frequently visit and read the welfare office, the courthouse, the jail, the military recruitment center, and the local elementary school. Perhaps we could also visit these places while reading scripture there together. This could happen in our seminary training, where we would also learn ways to continue this practice within a ministry assignment. Actually doing ministry in each setting may not be the work of every pastor, but we would be trained to expand our reading skills, and we would be given a deeper sense that this, too, is the turf of the church. Pastors are both congregational leaders and community leaders.

When Jesus walked onto the temple grounds during Holy Week, he did so with great authority. He did so with the authority of love, the authority of calling, and the strong belief that the political, economic, sociological, and certainly spiritual forces that converged in the temple complex were all relevant to the mission of the kingdom of God that he preached. He had read his missional context from the perch overlooking the city, he had felt it and perceived it deeply, and he engaged it with a sense of confident mission. This can be something toward which we aspire as a seminary and as a church: joyful, missional leadership that is good news to all creation.

Reflections on learning three

Marco Güete

The church and the seminary need to equip pastors and professors
to read and engage their missional contexts with joy.

This third learning helped me reflect on my own ministry—
and whether I have any joy in doing my ministry. It
was tremendous to reflect on this learning, particularly as
it pertains to my own life and ministry. This work not only
includes my reflection but also the reflections of some pastors
in the Southeast Mennonite Conference whom I asked to
contribute to the topic.

In the conference, we have pastors who are similar to any
other pastor in the rest of the denomination—they stay in a
church for five to nine years and then go to another church.
But we also have pastors who have been founders of congregations, and the congregations expect them to be in the

Marco Güete is Conference Minister for Southeast Mennonite Conference.
Marco participated in an Engaging Pastors–sponsored day of working together as
conference ministers and faculty in Pittsburgh in 2006 and the Engaging Pastors
Pastor-Faculty Colloquy for Area Church and Conference Ministers in 2007–08, and
he was involved in Seminario Bíblico Anabautista.

church forever—until they die or until the congregation dies. Some of my pastors are like that. I say to myself, well, they must have some kind of joy to do their ministry for all their lives—in the same place, serving the same people!

How does this learning resonate in your experience?

One of the questions posed to us was, how does this learning reasonate in your experience?

Seminary professors and pastors are first of all members of God's royal, prophetic, and priestly people in Christ (1 Pet. 2:4–5, 9). Christian leadership is distinctive for its servant nature (Luke 22:24–27; Mark 10:35–45), its particular character requirements (1 Tim. 3:2–7; Titus 1:7–9), and its source in the Holy Spirit (1 Cor. 12:7; Rom. 12:6–8). All Christians share in the witness of the church, and all have responsibility to do the work of the body of Christ during their lives, but scripture tells us that some are chosen to teach and others are chosen to lead. Teach whom? Lead whom? The answer is the other believers.

Professors in Mennonite theological seminaries today do their work for the enlightenment and guidance of God's people. They work first of all for the pastors who preach, teach, and pastor the church of Christ.

One of the pastors, Rick Lee, responded to my question in this way: "In my experience pastors who love people but do not like people are hard-pressed to engage—with joy. Allowing God to transform our hearts and our character to express God's own heart and character will enlighten and enliven us to his joy. The joy of the Lord is our strength. No joy, no strength. Little joy, little strength. Great joy, great strength."

What strikes you about this theme, and what ought we to pay attention to in it?

The other question asked of us was, what strikes you about this theme, and what ought we pay attention to in it? The church and the seminary have at least three essential duties to perform:

The **first duty** of the church and seminary is to be responsible for those who become professors in our Mennonite theological seminaries and pastors of our Mennonite churches. The church is to foster, guard, and defend this critical calling among the congregation members and to see that its candidates are properly trained, appointed, protected, and retained in their ministry. Is that a utopia? Maybe. Maybe not.

Richard MacMaster, who is one of the pastor's spouses and a retired professor and historian, reflects: "Robert Kreider once said to me that 'contagious enthusiasm' is the one thing a teacher has to offer. We all know of the really good teachers in our past who were excited about what they were teaching and helped us to 'catch' their enthusiasm. I have had teachers both in seminary and in my academic discipline who fit that definition (and some who didn't)."

A **second duty** of the church and the seminaries that care for Christ's church is to work in closest communion with professors and pastors, in order to learn from them by carefully, respectfully, and responsibly monitoring and questioning their study and teaching.

When I was writing and thinking about this part, my own context came to me. The majority of the pastors with whom I am working have not been to seminary. They are from other cultures, and they are new Mennonites. Also, members of the largest congregations in our denomination are not typical Mennonites.

Larry Diener, Associate Pastor of Bahia Vista Mennonite Church in Sarasota, Florida, had this to say:

> Not only do the church and the seminaries need to equip pastors and professors to read and engage their missional contexts with joy, but we also need to state and understand our missional contexts in such a way that they invite a joyful response...not only from our pastors and professors, but also from our students, our lay leaders, and the members of our congregations. When the missional context is inviting and exciting, it generates an enthusiastic and heartfelt response. Without the engagement of the heart with the mission, we end up driving instead of leading, coaxing instead of inviting, and pushing instead of drawing. May God grant us wisdom to better understand our call to the church and the world.

A recent issue of *Mennonite Weekly Review* related that being a pastor—a high-profile, high-stress job with nearly impossible expectations for success—can send one down the road of depression, according to pastoral counseling reports. Yet we are talking about joy. It is an amazing thing that a majority of the pastors responded that they have joy doing their ministry, even though they have a ton of problems and stress.

A **third duty** of the church and seminary is to mediate between the professors and the pastors. They do this by defending the respectability of Anabaptist Christian study, identity, and teaching on the highest scholarly level for those engaged in this work before and in behalf of the general members.

John Wierwille, Pastoral Elder at Berea Mennonite Church in Atlanta, Georgia, observes:

> The missional context is a forum in which the scriptures have been stripped of their challenge, condensed for easy consumption, and hijacked for political and cultural purposes. The promises of Christ stand in the face of most of the world and most of its ways. How does one stand against all the wrongs of the world with joy? Where is the source of our faith? Will we find it in the missional context? No. Maybe. Will we find it in the love and encouragement of all the congregations that have raised us up with the promises of the good news? Yes. Same as it ever was. Same as it will be. And thank God for that. Amen.

Reflections on my involvement in Engaging Pastors

Western District Conference, AMBS–Great Plains, and I took a risk in engaging Hispanic pastors and leaders in a new exploratory venture of theological training in Texas with the Seminario Bíblico Anabautista (Anabaptist Biblical Seminary) in Dallas. The Certificate in Theological Studies program has been established to provide the basics in Bible and theology for various Christian ministries. The program is designed for pastors, church planters, full-time or bivocational, and congregational leaders who have felt the call to Christian ministry.

For many of the pastors and leaders in Texas, the opportunity to study in the Dallas program is the only opportunity they have to study Mennonite theology at the seminary level in Spanish. Loren Johns, Associate Professor of New Testament at AMBS, states: "Thus, calling, training, and sustaining high quality pastoral leadership starts with something rather than nothing." The program has been quite modest and the effort is appreciated. In his report dated November 3, 2006, Jacob W. Elias tells the story of Esther Martinez, one of the enrolled pastors, who also served in a coordinating role for the weekend. Martinez put it this way: "Given our circumstances, most of us cannot come to AMBS. However, through this effort, we can have the seminary right here. This is a marvelous opportunity for us. Most of us are church planting pastors who are busy, since we also have to work for a living. Some of us have little more than a high school education. Yet this is affording us an opportunity for growth as ministering persons."

Reflections on learning three

David B. Miller

*The church and the seminary need to equip pastors and professors
to read and engage their missional contexts with joy.*

"The kingdom of heaven is like treasure hidden in a
field, which someone found and hid; who then in joy
goes and sells all and buys that field." (Matt. 13:44;
NRSV)

May the God of hope fill you with all joy and peace
in believing, so that you may abound in hope by the
power of the Holy Spirit. (Rom. 15:13; NRSV)

This, the third of the identified themes of the Engaging
Pastors project, is thick with meaning and possibility.
It suggests far more than a brief presentation may hope to
address. For this reason, I will limit my comments largely

David B. Miller is Associate Professor of Missional Leadership Development
at AMBS. Prior to fall 2009 David served as Pastor at University Mennonite Church
in State College, Pennsylvania. One of David's great joys is working with students
who are serving in ministry internships. He sees internships as a time of great discovery and growth and considers working with them a sacred privilege.

to the final prepositional phrase of the theme—a phrase that suggests that our missional engagement needs to be characterized by an essential emotive quality. That this quality is identified as joy is both striking and potentially transformative.

Permit me to share two brief encounters that occurred early in my experience as a pastor around twenty-five years ago. The first was an unannounced visit I made to a member of the congregation I was serving. On my way back from a meeting, I realized that I would pass the home of a member that I had not had opportunity to visit personally. This was before the advent of cell phones, so I made the stop unannounced. I arrived to find this brother working under the hood of his car. On seeing me, he apologized as he wiped grease off his hands. I said I was the one who owed the apology for stopping by without calling. As we talked he became noticeably uneasy. Finally he blurted out, "Dave, in my experience the minister never comes to call unless someone has died or sinned. I'm not aware of anyone dying, so is there something about which you've come to correct me?" He gave a sigh of relief when I told him my only agenda was to stop by and see where he lived and get better acquainted.

The second encounter was a couple of weeks later, following my first time leading a celebration of the Lord's Supper in a Mennonite congregation. In the service, I invited the congregation to approach the communion table "with joy." After the service, a kindly elder brother in the congregation told me that this was the first time that he had ever heard the word joy associated with communion. It had been, in his experience, a practice characterized by great angst, lest one should eat and drink "in an unworthy manner" (1 Cor. 11:27).

It seems to me that the identification of joy as an essential quality of our missional engagement has not been self-evident in Mennonite experience. It may be that joy has suffered suspicion in light of our critical analysis of both pietistic and charismatic traditions. Where there is too much joy, have we tended to suspect that serious obligations of discipleship have been lessened or even ignored? Yet the twin imperatives toward joy, rooted in both the biblical witness and the longing of the human soul, are too compelling and essential to ignore.

A cursory review of the principle term for joy in the New Testament instructs us that joy is:

- a gift and sign of God's Spirit,

- supremely grounded in the incarnation and resurrection,

- experienced in the present celebration of common faith and witness,

- communal in experience and expression,

- an emotional response to loving and being loved,

- persistent even in the face of suffering and difficulty,

- experienced both on earth and in heaven,

- eschatological in nature—experienced in present time in anticipation of its fullness being known in eternity.

Joy is both motivation for and response to faithful witness to Christ and the reign of God. As such, it is a Spirit-breathed emotional quality evidencing the interplay of divine initiative and human response, celebration, and participation.

One of the repeated observations contained in the reports from the Engaging Pastors project was the love of pastors for the congregations and persons that they have been called to serve. Such love is essential to joyful missional engagement. While it cannot be taught, both the church and seminary can contribute to fostering a "biblical realist" perspective on congregational life that will serve as a check on the frustration of this love and the diminishing of joy.

A biblical realist perspective remembers that the divine motivation for the incarnation is that "God so loved the world" and that "while we still were sinners, Christ died for us." This is not to reduce the incarnation to getting Jesus killed for our salvation, but to instill a deep remembrance that God is the initiator in love. Humanity—indeed, all of creation—in its present state is the object of God's love and redemptive action. God did not need to be appeased into such love, nor is the church so irresistibly attractive as to win God's love. Such biblical realism, particularly among pastors, is a safeguard against being so enamored of one's idealized vision of the faithful church that one despises the church as it is. In such realism is the transforming release from the myth of our own goodness.

The "with joy" clause at the end of this theme is a reminder that the work of this theme has to do first with spiritual formation. To such formation may and ought to be added the skills needed to "read and engage their missional context." Such skills as competency in understanding social contexts of congregations and ministry are significant, but without the transforming work that is the source of joy, they are too easily reduced to technique that is neither life-giving nor attractive.

Joy as a fruit of the Spirit, when released in human rela-
tions, is a positive contagion that readily spreads from one
person or group to another. The church's missional engagement, while both alert to and critical of the way that the fallen
powers have distorted and marred the image of God, must
be well formed by God's Spirit to witness with joy to the
kingdom coming. Such joy is renewed in worship, celebrated
in fellowship, and extended in service.

Reflections on learning three

Lois Barrett

The church and the seminary need to equip pastors and professors
to read and engage their missional contexts with joy.

As I read the reports of the Listening Project, the issue of contexts came up frequently, particularly the variety of contexts in which AMBS graduates serve. They said:

AMBS needs to know that AMBS is preparing students for a variety of pastoral situations.

The AMBS curriculum should be more intentional about alerting students to the variety of congregational contexts and styles.

AMBS needs programs and courses that equip students to be aware of the surrounding culture in which congregations exist, the distinctive congregational

Lois Barrett is Director of AMBS–Great Plains and Associate Professor of Theology and Anabaptist Studies. Lois participated in an Engaging Pastors Seminary Course Revision and two Listening Projects and gave oversight to Seminario Bíblico Anabautista.

culture, and how the church engages its cultural environment.

There is a need for courses and pastoral theologies that not only "make room" for alternative models of ministry, but that prepare students for ministry in such contexts.

AMBS needs to understand that rural churches can be missional.

We need to give attention to shifting cultural values and how that affects the way we do church.

Another recent graduate said that at AMBS he learned to think carefully about how the gospel intersects with culture. He gained greater understanding about the church itself as a cultural entity that both accommodates itself to and differentiates itself from the surrounding culture. Another said that there needs to be an "awareness of the distinctive congregational culture and how the church engages its cultural environment—as well as its location on the continuum between a separatist ethic or spiritual ethos, on the one end, and an assimilated reality, on the other." Yet another graduate desired more tools for reading all the multiple contexts that one encounters in ministry, with the recognition that cookie-cutter models do not work well. "We need a religious anthropologist."

How do people learn to read their contexts? How can church leaders approach every congregation's setting as a mission field?

Joy of discovery

A missional worldview requires an understanding of culture and context. The gospel is always contextual; the gospel is always embedded in a culture. Even scriptures are written in and to particular contexts, and the story of the early church is one of the gospel being embedded in Gentile as well as Jewish cultures. There is no context-less gospel—some set of abstract principles that can simply be translated into any language. Gospel—good news—is a narrative, a narrative set in particular contexts and cultures but able to be embodied in multiple contexts and cultures.

Because there is no gospel without context, proclaimers and demonstrators of the gospel must look at the dominant culture in the West in the same way we have been taught to look at cultures of the East and of the South or of more recent immigrant groups in North America. No culture is exempt from this scrutiny.

But the attention paid to context does not mean that the church assimilates into the culture. We want to avoid syncretism. Being contextual is not an all-or-nothing proposition. The church can only be a witness within a culture when it is different from that culture for the sake of the gospel.

What is needed is a way to discern what of the culture is consistent with the gospel or neutral and what is counter to the gospel. Steve Bevans calls this the "countercultural" model of contextualization. I like the language of Paul Hiebert, who names this method "critical contextualization." If the church can read the culture and discern it well, this is the joy of discovery.

Joy of communication

If we have discovered our contexts, we have the opportunity to communicate the gospel to people in those contexts. The issue of communication also came up in the Listening Project reports:

> Is there another way to reach out to people, not waiting for them to enter the doors of the church?

> Apologetics is critical in postmodernity, where faith cannot be assumed and where it must be justified or explained.

Another pastor was deeply concerned about the missional role of the church, especially in communicating it in a congregational context filled with insider language and a lack of enthusiasm for personal evangelism. Another recent graduate hoped seminaries would help students communicate the gospel across cultural boundaries, including those in this country.

Faith sharing is a practice—a habitual behavior practiced by a community over time. It is learned—and improved—by practicing it. Sometimes people in congregations have problems sharing their faith even with others in the same congregation, so it is there that practicing must begin, along with listening to others share their faith. Then we can begin the practice in more diverse contexts, remembering that communication is complete only when the message is received. When we do this well, we experience the joy of communication.

Joy of transformation

What changes are needed for us to receive this joy? For seminaries? For area and churchwide organizations? For congregations?

Change does not happen simply by increasing the number of our exhortations. We need to understand change processes in relation to worldviews. According to Paul Hiebert in the recently published book *Transforming Worldviews*, we can look at cultures in terms of patterns of behavior and experiences, or signs and rituals. But at a deeper level, culture is about belief systems. At a deeper level yet is worldview. Hiebert cites Edward Hall, who asserts that worldview is "a set of unspoken, implicit rules of behavior and thought." It is the "hidden cultural grammar that defines the way people view the world."[1] It tells us the categories in which we can think, the questions it is possible to ask, and the logic by which it is possible to know.

When we look at faith transformation, we consider not only change in behaviors and beliefs, but change in worldview. An example of such a change would be a shift from understanding truth as only what one can perceive with the five senses or figure out through reason, to understanding truth as also coming through the spiritual world.

When we look at congregational or organizational transformation, missional change is also connected with worldview. Such change is not simply a new program or a new set of tools but a shift in worldview. All congregational change

---

1. Edward Hall, *Hidden Differences: How to Communicate with the Germans*, Studies in International Communication (Hamburg: Stern, 1983), 6–7, quoted in *Transforming Worldviews*, by Paul Hiebert (Grand Rapids, MI: Baker Academic, 2008), 32.

processes and tools are contextual and products of world-views. There are no theologically or contextually neutral tools. Our worldview shapes the questions we ask, the questions we think are possible, and the courses it occurs to us to teach.

For AMBS this might mean more intentionally preparing Master of Divinity students for a variety of contexts and helping them understand those contexts. It might mean teaching how to discern what parts of the surrounding culture can be vehicles for the gospel and what parts need to be opposed.

My hope is that seminary, conferences, and churches may think well, wisely, and diligently about a missional worldview in our various contexts and experience the joy of transformation.

Report on learning three

Listening Committee

The church and the seminary need to equip pastors and professors to read and engage their missional contexts with joy.

Resonance with learning three

- There was a fairly consistent affirmation of learning three.

- There was a strong affirmation of the phrase "with joy," as it points toward the spiritual aspects of this learning.

- Yet there was some question about why the learning calls for joy instead of grace, hope, peace, or another fruit of the Spirit, keeping in mind that joy is one part of a fuller spectrum that may include sorrow.

- Joy helps us move beyond disillusionment and despair; joy will be evidence of hope.

- Joy is fundamental and attractive; we can share our faith with joy and integrity.

Emerging themes

- We must look at the ecology of ministry comprehensively, including some parts that aren't represented here (for example, Mennonite Central Committee, Mennonite Economic Development Associates, interim pastors).

- Seminaries train, but it falls to area church and conference ministers to cultivate soil for missional engagement.

- In Luke 10, the seventy disciples returned with joy after a trip into the field; missional engagement and joy feed each other.

- There was a lot of affirmation of AMBS's efforts to educate all students to be leaders for God's reconciling mission in the world.

- Engaging a multicultural world should be part of the seminary curriculum.

- There is a need for area church/conference ministers and professors who are missional leaders.

- The learning puts pastors and professors at the same place in the sentence; both are engaging respective missional contexts, and yet the discussion has focused almost exclusively on the pastors.

- One polarity at work is the necessity to be different from our context and yet inhabit it.

- The Holy Spirit is leading us, which gives us the freedom to take risks.

Significant questions

- Does too much focus on our contexts put us at risk of losing sight of the church's mission?

- In what ways are the skills for reading our contexts the same as skills for reading the text? In what ways do they differ?

- Rather than reading and engaging contexts (which implies some detachment and an us/them dichotomy), what would it mean to *inhabit* our context?

- What is the role of church agencies in this process, as well as Mennonite Central Committee? How do we honor existing partnerships and continue to collaborate with our current partners?

- Do we need a specialist to teach engagement with missional contexts, or is such teaching spread across the curriculum?

- Who is teaching whom?

Trajectories and suggestions

- There is a need to develop a theology of learning from failure so that it's okay to take risks, which is a necessity when engaging in missional activity.

- We must learn to lead change and transformation.

- Pastors need to be taught skills of sociological analysis.

- The credentialing process is a strategic opportunity we must take advantage of. Might there be a way to include continuing education unit (CEU) requirements for missional and leadership training?

- Could seminaries put staff on the ground to help clusters of churches train church planters?

- Could seminaries create an advisory council of pastors and middle judicatory leadership to help connect the seminaries with the broader church?

- Established and emerging churches could be paired to foster a broader understanding of their respective contexts; engaging a new context sends us back to our own contexts with new eyes.

- Seminary internships should include a focus on context and missional vision.

Musings by the Listening Committee

- Let's be willing to make new mistakes in going forward.

- What if we made creativity, innovation, and risk—rather than success—the measures of a good leader?

- Let us neither dismiss the wisdom of including the word *joy* in the learning, nor be distracted by discussion about whether it was the best choice, lest we miss the heart of the learning.

Stepping into a shared future
Fleeting thoughts on the Summative Conference

Rebecca Slough

I try not to let my hopes get too high for anything, particularly special events. My imagination is active, and I begin anticipating all sorts of amazing possibilities, extraordinary wonders, unspeakable ecstasies. . . . Then the real thing comes and goes, and mostly I'm disappointed. The experience falls far short of my wild imaginings.

But not this time.

The Engaging Pastors Summative Conference was all that I could have hoped for—committed, passionate people who love Christ and his church, who respect one another's work, who care about current and future colleagues in ministry and align themselves with God's work in the world. Oh,

---

Rebecca Slough is Academic Dean and Associate Professor of Worship and the Arts at AMBS. Rebecca believes that "good pastors are artists who improvise countless variations on the theme of God's saving work in Jesus Christ and the inauguration of his reign." She says, "I thrill to watch students, colleagues, and even strangers risk the transforming possibilities of improvisation."

and we also have the gifts of wisdom, imagination, and gab. The rich insights of our presentations, working groups, and Listening Committee reports gave us more than any one of us could possibly absorb.

From my vantage point in the dean's office at AMBS, several large issues emerged from the Summative Conference and the Engaging Pastors project broadly, and to address them will require all of us in the ministerial ecology of Mennonite Church Canada and Mennonite Church USA.

1. Currently we do not have the communication or the organizational structures in place in our denominations to continue the kinds of discussion and imaging that made the Summative Conference so valuable. For two days we practiced a discipline of open listening and conversation, the kind of discipline that will be required if our common purpose is shaping and sustaining missional leadership for the church. Mennonite Church Canada is beginning to imagine new possibilities in this regard, with its strategic task force on leadership education.

   AMBS professors would benefit from and contribute greatly to regular (perhaps yearly?) engagements with pastors, conference or area church ministers, denominational leaders, and theological educators in our sister schools. Who else is ready to put time and resources into conversations that will strengthen the ministry ecology of our church?

2. The Summative Conference displayed our complex feelings about pastoral authority. Differences within our racial/ethnic communities increase the complexity. I won-

der whether it is time for further conversations on the nature, character, and purpose of authority for all who are called to participate in God's work in the world. Perhaps examining the authority of all believers serving in ministry, wherever they are, could shed a different light on expressions of authority that are unique to pastoral leadership. By what or whose authority do any of us act? Is authority connected to our baptism? What or who is the source of authority for those in the priesthood of all believers? Who or what is the source of pastoral authority? Might such questions open some new avenues of theological reflection on authority in a missional church?

Some AMBS professors and students are interested in taking up the discernment of such questions. Who are the pastors, church leaders, and other educators willing to work on a more holistic understanding of ministry, leadership, and authority?

3. Claire Wolfteich's presentation has caused me to ponder the kinds of peer relationships, continuing education, and spiritual practices that sustain pastors in their ministry. She did not focus her presentation on joy (the word we discussed related to our third learning), but surely the way that pastors continue to grow opens new space for God's Spirit to harvest the fruits of gratitude, peace, and hope, as well as joy. What helps Mennonite pastors remain open to the Spirit's fruitful work? What role might AMBS and our sister schools play in supporting growth in ministry long after pastors have completed their formal ministry education programs? How might we plan

our continuing education curriculum, mentoring relationships, and peer support groups to effectively use the resources the church has given to us?

4. A number of years ago, when I was teaching at another school, I met a second-career student on the day he sold his carpentry equipment—the tools he had used daily in his first career. It was a hard day for him. While he felt called to pastoral ministry—and was pastoring in the congregation that had called him—he was sad and more than a little afraid. The seminary had provided him a needed place of stability as he transitioned from being a carpenter into being a pastor. Transition into ministry—whether from school to congregation or an occupation into pastoral leadership—is difficult. No single congregation, school, or conference can provide the support needed to make such a transition.

The Summative Conference was one of my first glimpses of hope that our emerging ecology of ministry may be becoming robust enough to help new pastors transition into ministry. Muriel Bechtel of Mennonite Church Eastern Canada and Marianne Mellinger of Conrad Grebel University College are forging a Transition into Ministry program we all could learn from. Other schools and denominations are experimenting with additional models we should explore.

Should the transition into ministry happen after students complete their programs, or could a third year be completed while they serve the congregation to which they have been called? How could theological education begin when pastors are called from their congregations and start with little or no formal ministerial education? How do the processes of licensing and ordination support the process of transitioning into ministry? Is it true that congregations, conferences, ministry educational programs, and the denominations are all stakeholders when someone is licensed or ordained for ministry? If so, could this process intentionally draw in the other stakeholders in a meaningful way?

5. The last session of the Summative Conference demonstrated the kind of creativity we need to cultivate in order to address the kinds of questions I've identified above. I'm not sure we've started the revolution quite yet. I'm still searching for the deeper meanings of "Dropkick Me, Jesus"—here my imagination has been greatly stretched. Yet, some of the embodied images and the poetry captured me more than all the words we offered one another.

I suspect that the ongoing process of strengthening our ministry ecology will be a bit like health-care reform in the United States. No one grand plan will provide all the solutions required. Initiatives for change will be local and regional; others might be structural, changing the way that we relate with one another over a period of time. Some of our attempts at collaboration will succeed beyond our wildest dreamings; others will fail miserably.

One outcome of the Summative Conference that I hope stays with us all for a long time is the feeling of collegiality and mutual support we offered to one another. It is my prayer that none of us will go about our work without considering what we might have to learn from other colleagues serving in congregations, those working in regional or conference leadership, and those teaching in our schools or leading our denominations. None of us alone has the best answer for how to sustain effective and joy-filled missional leadership. We need one another in order to discern the future that God has for Mennonite Church USA and Mennonite Church Canada.

For ourselves and for the church, I pray that we may know a deeper love for Jesus, greater passion for the ministry to which we have been called, boundless trust in the Spirit's guidance, more imaginative creativity in our work, with goodwill and respect for one another as servant leaders of God's reign.